Developing Literacy Naturally

Lyndon W. Searfoss, Ph.D.
Arizona State University
Thomas W. Bean, Ph.D.
University of Nevada–Las Vegas
Jeffrey I. Gelfer, Ph.D.
University of Nevada–Las Vegas

KENDALL/HUNT PUBLISHING COMPANY
4050 Westmark Drive   Dubuque, Iowa 52002

Top left and bottom right cover photos by Susan Johns and Gary Meader.
Top right cover photo by PhotoDisc.
Bottom left cover photo by Corel.

Interior photographs by Susan Johns and Gary Meader.

Contents

PREFACE

Young children have a natural interest and excitement about language and literacy. Our book is designed to help you nurture young children's literacy development in day care, preschools, kindergartens, and primary grade classrooms.

Our approach to young children's literacy development includes how to design and manage effective classroom environments, centers, and theme-based teaching and learning. In addition, we included resources and suggestions for working with second language learners, strategies for inclusion, and building parent partnerships.

Throughout the book, we relied on our own classroom experiences as well as those of other teachers, our students, and our families. We hope you find our ideas helpful as you work with young children.

LWS
TWB
JIG

ACKNOWLEDGMENTS

Special thanks goes to Nancy Bean whose practical experiences with teaching young children proved invaluable in the development of this book. Nancy's sharp editorial eye kept children at the center of our writing.

Two of the best kindergarten teachers we know, Betty Gernant and Ann Poole, provided us with inspiration and reminded us, by example, that if you expect the best from children, that's what you get.

Margaret Greer Jewell and the late Miles V. Zintz through their text, *Learning to Read and Write Naturally* (1990), also published by Kendall/Hunt, was a source of ideas for this text especially in how to create and manage classroom environments.

Thanks also to our graduate students, Judy Baumgarten and Sandy Pontillas at the University of Nevada - Las Vegas and Beth Jones and Cory Hansen at Arizona State University, for their assistance in collecting ideas and materials for this book.

Finally, Jeff Gelfer wants to thank Peggy G. Perkins for her loving support and their son, Sacha D. Gelfer, who was more than patient at all times. Jeff also credits his parents with giving him the wonderful gift of a love of learning.

CHAPTER 1

An Introduction to Developing Literacy Naturally

In the children's book, *The sand horse* (Turnbull, 1989), an artist who creates animals in the sand makes a beautiful, galloping horse at the beach. At sunset, the artist goes home and the sand horse magically wakes up. The horse wants to join the windswept "white horses" (white caps) churning the water far out at sea. As the tide slowly rolls over the sand horse, he joins his friends galloping across the ocean, far offshore and free.

For very young children, even objects like the sand horse are magical and alive. "A young child can enter the world of story as easily as Cinderella stepping into the pumpkin carriage" (Wolf & Heath, 1992, p.1). Watch any baby in a stroller and you will see eyes glued to your face, checking you out, and moving on to study the rattles or other toys that hang all around the stroller. You and the rattles are alive and exciting to the young child. People's unique faces, the sound or laughter of another voice, or the pages of a cloth book are all exciting contacts with adults to young children.

Learning, especially about how to use language, is in high gear for very young children. Your position in child care, whether you work in a public, private or "mom and pop" daycare center, preschool or elementary school, provides a rare chance to be a crucial figure in a child's language learning. Children make very rapid gains in language learning, especially if they are in caring, stimulating environments where their coos, babbles, scribbles with crayons, and interest in

Figure 1.1. Shannon, 2½ years

stories are each valued and encouraged. Just look quickly through Figures 1 through 6 in this chapter to see children's writing move from simple pictures expressing emotions (see Figure 1.1 for a day that wasn't going too well for Shannon, age 2½), to experiments with letters (Figure 1.2), to early stories only they can tell you about (Figure 1.3), family news events (Figure 1.4), and longer pieces of writing (Figures 1.5 and 1.6).

More infants, toddlers, and preschoolers find themselves in child care settings than ever before in

Children become part of the stories they read.

Figure 1.2. Kristen, 4¹/₂ years

our country. These settings can begin a child's successful journey in learning to read and to write. *Simply put, while children are away from home in your care, what you do to encourage talking and writing, and by reading to them, you will make a difference in their language development.*

This book is full of ideas for how you can organize exciting learning environments where young children can explore talking, reading, and writing. In *Chapter Two: Infants, Toddlers and Daycare Settings for Literacy Development*, we consider infant and toddler daycare settings. While your role as a care-giver is important at all stages of a young child's development, you are truly an infant and toddler's security blanket when it comes to feeling safe and "okay" while away from home. In this chapter, we recommend a variety of cloth books and stories to read to infants and toddlers that they will enjoy.

Chapter Three: Developing Effective Preschool Environments, shows you how to create preschool environments that use children's natural curiosity about language and print. Young children are surrounded by print on television, in stores, advertisements, and

The caregiver is a child's security blanket away from home.

Preschool environments should surround children with oral language and print.

Figure 1.3. I went to Fun Factory. Alex, 5½ years

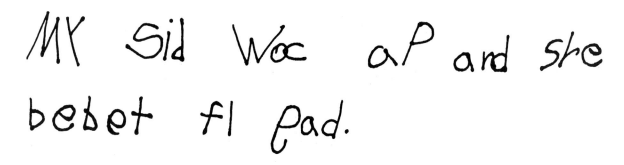

Figure 1.4. My sister woke up and she barfed in bed. Mari, 6 years

so on. Effective preschool environments build on children's print awareness by labeling items in activity centers and surrounding children with all kinds of oral language and print. The alphabet, children's names, and lots of books make this an ideal age for developing literacy naturally. Songs, rhymes, and imaginative play all serve to boost children's language development. In Chapter Three, we introduce a unit on ants that shows the range of language and other creative activities possible in preschool settings as children learn about the world of ants. We also demonstrate how to organize centers and schedule a unit.

Chapter Four: Kindergarten and Emerging Literacy, explores life in kindergarten, where just like flowers, children begin to bloom as readers and writers. In this chapter we introduce half-day and full-day kindergarten schedules with many language activities for you to try. Centers, introduced in the preschool chapter, are expanded in the kindergarten classroom. We also present ways to teach reading and writing and simple and informal assessments appropriate for kindergarten children.

Chapter Five: First Grade and Beyond, moves into first grade and beyond where young children will continue to emerge as readers and writers, each on their own time table. In this chapter we introduce mini-lessons and teaching strategies aimed at guiding children both toward a love of literacy and the skills and strategies they will need as readers and writers. We also help you plan and manage classroom instruction.

Chapters Six through Chapter Nine each consider a special issue. *Chapter Six: Inclusion: Literacy Development for All Children,* presents ways to ensure all children are included in learning environments. *Chapter Seven: Assessing Early Literacy Through Portfolios,* shows how to use portfolios to collect samples of children's language learning. *Chapter Eight: Second Language Learners,* provides ways to help second language learners grow and develop. Finally, *Chapter Nine: Parent Involvement,* offers ways for parents and other caregivers to continue their role as children's "first teachers" and become your partners in helping children develop literacy naturally.

Throughout our book, we express the viewpoint that children are active learners. The foundation for becoming successful readers and writers begins with infants and toddlers and is linked to the quality of care they receive. On the other hand, "Research reveals that children who fail to develop proficiency in language during the first years of life are up to six times more likely to experience reading problems after they go to school" (Boyer, 1996, p. 2). Clearly, as you already know, your role in shaping children's lives is an important one. As you explore the strategies in our book, we hope we can add to what you already know about helping children develop literacy naturally.

We also invite you to tell us how you used the ideas in our book, the ones you found helpful and the ones that just did not seem right for you and your children. Contact us by mail at the addresses on the back cover of this book or through the Kendall/Hunt Publishing Company web site at: http://www.kendallhunt.com. We would really enjoy hearing from you!

Children are active learners!

References

Boyer, E. L. (1996). Literacy and learning. In M. F. Graves, P. Van Den Brook, & B. M. Taylor (Eds.), *The first R: Every child's right to read.* New York: Teachers College Press.

Turnbull, A. (1989). *The sand horse.* New York: Athenaeum.

Wolf, S. A., & Heath, S. B. (1992). *The braid of literature: Children's worlds of reading.* Cambridge, MA: Harvard University Press.

Lyn Searfoss
Tom Bean
Jeff Gelfer

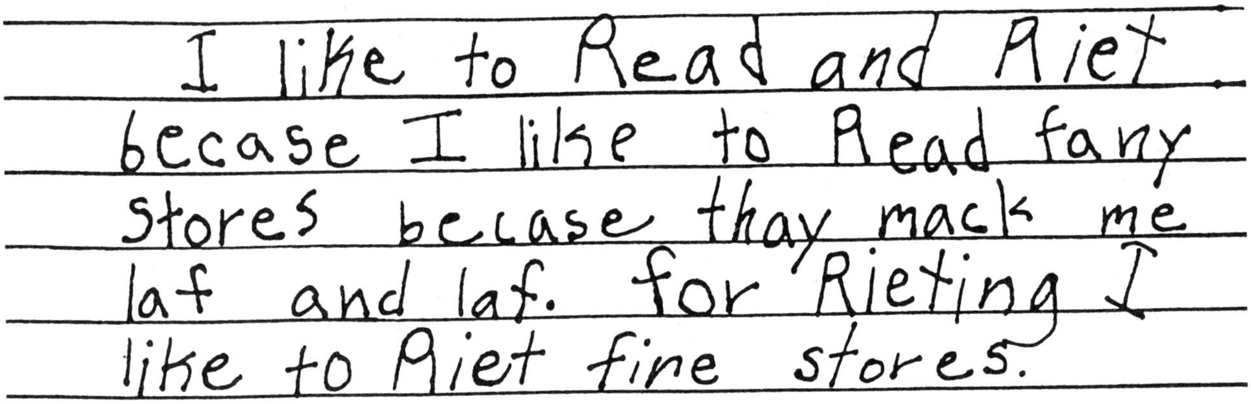

I like to Read and Riet becase I like to Read fany stores becase thay mack me laf and laf. for Rieting I like to Riet fine stores.

Figure 1.5. Chris, 7 years

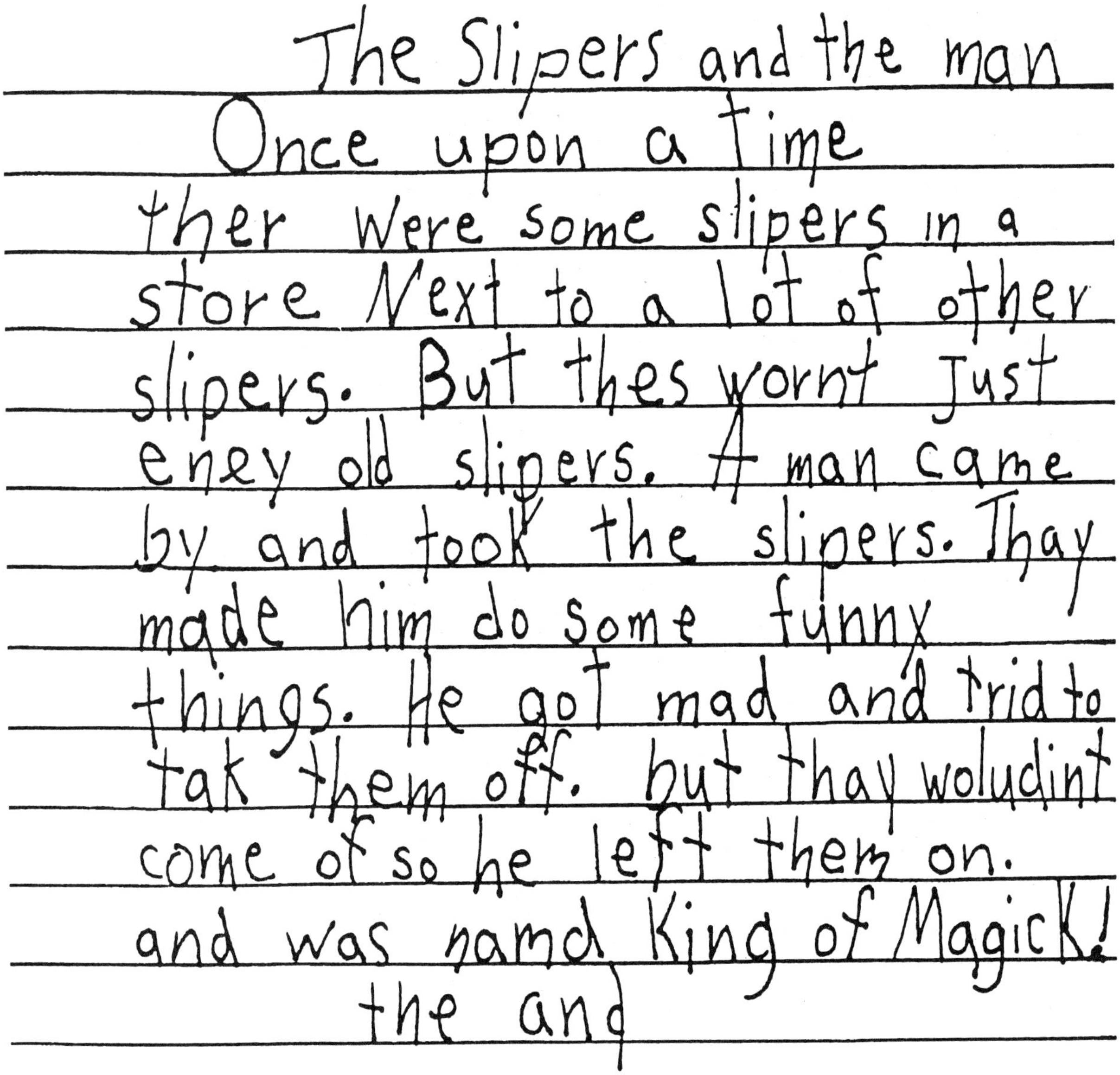

The Slipers and the man
Once upon a Time ther were some slipers in a store Next to a lot of other slipers. But thes wornt Just eney old slipers. A man came by and took the slipers. Thay made him do some funny things. He got mad and trid to tak them off. but thay woludint come of so he left them on. and was namd King of Magick! the and

Figure 1.6. Julie, 8 years

CHAPTER 2

Infants, Toddlers, and Day Care Settings for Literacy Development

COUNTRY DAY CARE CENTER

Mom rushes in the door with four-month-old Joey on one shoulder and a gigantic diaper bag on her other shoulder. Miss Jacobs calls out "Good morning, Joey." Joey grins and watches Miss Jacobs as his mom makes her way to the refrigerator where she unpacks four bottles and a lunch box from her diaper bag. She then drops off her diaper bag in Joey's cubby, signs the role sheet, checks the parent note board and takes Joey over to Miss Jacobs.

"Joey was up two times last night. I think he might be cutting a tooth," she tells Miss Jacobs. "I had to wake him up to bring him here so he might need a long nap."

"Hi Joey," says Miss Jacobs and she puts out her hands to take Joey. Joey hesitates and then reaches out to Miss Jacobs.

"You're not feeling too good today, huh? Well, we'll have to watch out for you today. Let's say goodbye to Mommy now." Joey waves goodbye and Miss Jacobs tells him, "I have a special toy to show you today." Miss Jacobs turns Joey away from his mother while she leaves the room and sits down on the floor to play with him and his special toy.

Families increasingly rely on day care settings to provide safe, nurturing childcare for their infants and toddlers while at work. Childcare options range from day care centers to in-home relative and non-relative nannies and au pairs (Howes & Hamilton, 1993). The quality of day care an infant or toddler experiences is crucial because very young children form attachments with care givers that influence their physical, social, and psychological development (Howes & Hamilton, 1993). In one early childhood education policy study (Kamerman & Kahn, 1995), the authors put it this way:

> Although all stages of life have significant implications for development and none should be ignored, no other period is as important as these first three years in setting the stage for an individual's ability to thrive physically, to learn, to love, to trust others, to develop the capacity for productive work, and to develop confidence...(p. 4)

In this chapter we take you through typical infant and toddler day care settings with an emphasis on what you can do to foster the natural development of children's language and interest in literacy. Books we have found that attract an infant or toddler's attention are introduced. We pay special attention in this chapter to health and safety concerns that you need to follow when you are working in day care settings. We offer a list of additional resources and books you may wish to read to gather further information on

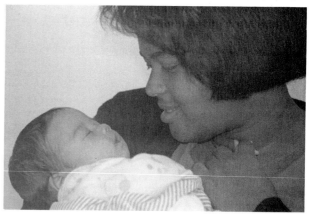

Very young children form strong attachments with their caregivers.

working with infants and toddlers, along with professional organizations you may find helpful.

We have divided the chapter into two major sections: (a) infants, and (b) toddlers as each has special concerns. The section on infants focuses on children from birth to twelve months. The section on toddlers looks at one to two year-olds.

INFANTS

Much of your work with infants in day care centers will be devoted to comforting babies left in your care. Infants need to feel happy and secure so that learning can take place. Picking up and holding crying babies, changing diapers and feeding, playing, touching, and cuddling babies are what a responsive caregiver does (Kamerman & Kahn, 1995).

While it may appear that you are spending all your time physically caring for infants, it is during these tasks that you have a great opportunity to expand an infant's language development. At this young age, you will be working on developing infants' playful use of oral language, which will help in their further language and literacy learning. Your response to infants' babbling makes them feel their *talk* is important and this will encourage more oral language play.

Infants enjoy hearing adults talk, read, and sing. Games like pat-a-cake and peekaboo fascinate infants (Morrow, 1997). Here are some general guidelines that give you an idea of what infants do with language and literacy (Morrow, 1997).

Language

1. Infants play with sounds at six months.
2. Their babbling becomes more involved as they combine consonant sounds with vowel sounds: "Ba, Ba, Ba....."

3. Infants say their first words between about eight and twelve months.
4. By two years of age a child may have a vocabulary of up to 150 words.

Literacy

1. A four to five month-old infant usually enjoys games like pat-a-cake.
2. Reading to an infant from birth to three months will sometimes captivate a baby's interest and other times be ignored by the baby.
3. Interest in listening to an adult reading grows during the period from three to six months.

The way a day care setting is organized and how you work in that setting will influence infants' language and literacy development. You, the teacher or caregiver is the most important asset a day care setting has. The lower the child-teacher ratio the more attention and learning the child receives. In the section that follows, we offer guidelines for a safe, healthy, and nurturing environment for language and literacy growth.

INFANT DAY CARE CLASSROOM SETTING

The layout of a safe and nurturing classroom setting is illustrated in Figure 2.1.

Overall Layout

Cribs should line one wall so that the infants are visible to the teacher at all times whether the children are awake or asleep. The wall can be lined with childsafe plastic mirrors along the crib wall at the infants' level when in the crib. Walls and ceilings around the babies should be colorful. Cribs with built-in drawers or cupboards and shelves provide storage for children's things (extra clothes, spare diapers, wipes, and so on). These drawers or cupboards also prevent crawling babies from going under the cribs.

Diaper Changing Area

The diaper changing area is an important part of the infant day care setting. Efforts must be made to maintain sanitary and safe conditions. The changing table should face the classroom so you do not have to

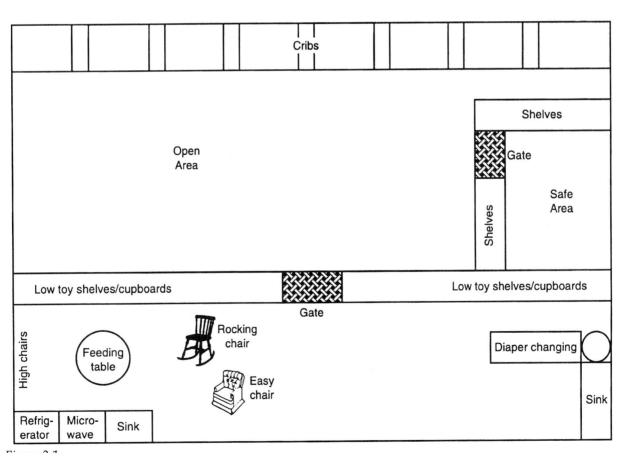

Figure 2.1.

turn your back on the rest of the children. This should also be a time and place where infants find enjoyment in language play. Figure 2.2 displays a diaper changing arrangement. The floor should be made of material that is easy to clean. This area should be off limits to infants.

The table should have a changing pad of some kind which can be easily disinfected or a paper which is changed with each diapering. A spray solution which is kept in a shelf above the changing table out of infants reach should be sprayed on the pad and wiped with a disposable paper towel after each diaper change. The table should have an edge around it to prevent the baby from rolling off. An infant should never be left unattended on the table!

There should be a cubby for each child either above or below the table containing each child's diapers, wipes, powder, change of clothes, and so on. The cubby should be reachable from the table so you can reach this with your hand still securing the child. Each child should have his own supplies to prevent the spread of illnesses. Plastic bags should be available in which to place soiled clothes, and a permanent marker

Reading to an infant may captivate the baby's interest.

Figure 2.2

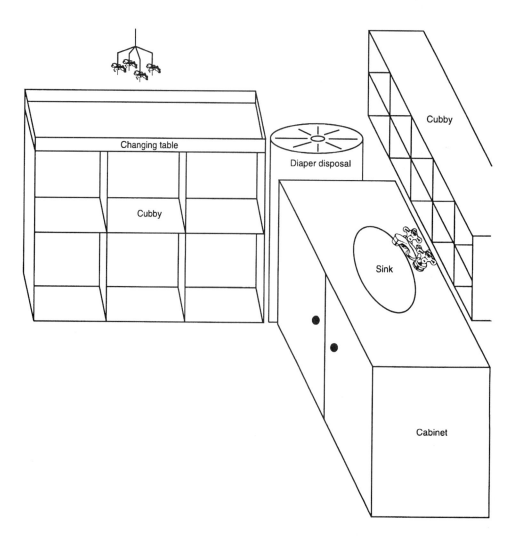

should be used to label plastic bags with the child's name. Shelves at the changing area need to be re-stocked every day either before or after school, or before each changing so that when you begin diaper changing you will not have to leave the area.

The diaper disposal container should be next to the changing table. You must be able to dispose of diapers without leaving the child. The containers should have a secure lid to prevent odors from escaping. The lid should also be easy for the teacher to open.

A sink should be located next to the diaper changing table for handwashing. This sink should not be used for food preparation or clean up.

Steps in Diaper Changing

1. Place the baby on the table
2. Retrieve all items needed for changing
3. Change baby according to parental directions (e.g. use of powder, wipes, ointment and so on)
4. Dispose of diaper and put dirty clothes in bag
5. Return child to crib
6. Return diapering items to child's cubby including any soiled clothes to be returned home
7. Disinfect area
8. Wash hands with disinfecting soap

Diaper changing should be a fun time for the baby. Infants have your devoted attention during this time. This is a great time for you to encourage language development. Here are some ideas of things to talk about with the infant on the changing table:

1. Sing or recite nursery rhymes
2. Point to mobiles or pictures and label them
3. Talk about and label infant's body parts
4. Count fingers, toes, arms, and so on
5. Peek-a-boo

Feeding Area

Feeding infants takes a considerable amount of your time in a typical day care setting. Feeding should be a fun time with lots of talking and singing as you interact with the child. Small infants requiring bottles should be held and fed in rocking chairs or comfortable easy chairs. Rocking easy chairs are ideal for infants and child care workers. You will need a refrigerator, microwave oven, and a sink.

Bottles filled with formula, and water or juice should be provided and prepared by the parents.

You will need multiple high chairs or feeding tables for hand feeding of infants and toddlers. They should all have a means of securing the child in the chair using a belt or harness for safety. The child's food should

be prepared by the parents at home and require no more than heating by the teacher. Solid dishes are the parents' responsibility to clean. You can probably handle hand-feeding three children at a time. Children should be encouraged to feed themselves whenever possible using finger foods. This will make your job easier and it is good for children to learn how to feed themselves.

Infant Safe Area

Although we argue for a stimulating infant environment with lots of talk, things to watch and touch, and books to listen to, you should also have a safe play area that is carpeted and free of anything that could harm a baby. This is a place in the day care center where you can leave an infant and know that he/she will come to no harm. This does not mean the infant should be unsupervised, but there are times when you will be occupied with other children, meals, or parents and you will need a place like this. Toys should be carefully selected for safety. This can also be an area to separate the non-crawling infants from the mobile toddlers.

Health and safety are major concerns with infants so cleanliness is very important. Everything goes into the child's mouth. Toys should be cleaned at the close of each day. Special attention should be paid when selecting your toys to ensure they can be cleaned easily.

The large open play area is where most of the infants' active play will occur. It should contain at least one easy chair for you to sit with a baby and talk, play, read, or cuddle. There should be blankets to lay on the floor for the non-crawling infants. There should be a variety of toys in this area that are all infant safe. For example, some of the toys that would be okay here include:

1. Rattles and noise makers
2. Dolls and stuffed animals
3. Large toys to push and pull
4. Large blocks for the early walker to pull-up on
5. Toys of different textures and colors
6. Cloth or baby safe books

This area is also where you should introduce or teach new things to children. Teaching at this age is a one-on-one experience. Remember that you, the teacher are the most important thing in the room to the infant.

Repetition at this age is important too. Infants love to hear the same book read over and over, as they like to listen to the rhythm of Mother Goose and other stories. They like to see familiar items and will master a

Teaching at this age is a one-on-one experience.

simple puzzle with repeated tries. Therefore, you need to introduce new items into this area periodically, but keep a lot of the old familiar items, too.

The most important thing to an infant or toddler is the teacher or caregiver. A small child needs to feel secure, comfortable, loved, and happy before learning can happen. Give the children in your care all the hugs they need and they will blossom. This is especially important when a child starts out in your care. Some children will feel secure in a couple of days. Others will take weeks. If you have to give up your

teaching activity because Ben needs to be held all day, then forget the activity. It is better to spend the day teaching Ben that you care and he will be okay. In fact, you will be teaching Ben as you spend time talking to him, reading to him, singing to him, and playing games with him. As Ben begins to feel secure in your presence he will want to get down and play. Or, he will fall asleep and you can put him down in his crib. Most importantly, Ben will begin to feel safe and loved in his new home away from home and that is when learning can begin.

Children need to feel loved and happy.

In the section that follows, we discuss toddler environments which, in many ways, resemble infant environments but with the added dimension of mobility. Toddlers can explore a greater range of territory in a day care setting. You can build on their early language and literacy experiences using this new found ability to move and explore.

Tiny Town Nursery School

Mary is doing her best to sit still in her car seat, but she's already played with all the toys she can reach. She starts pushing on the restraints but cannot budge it.

"We'll be at Miss Judy's in a minute," says Dad.

"Doo Dee, Doo Dee" (Judy, Judy) says Mary.

They are finally at Tiny Town Nursery School. Dad gets Mary out of her car seat. While balancing Mary on his hip, he retrieves the diaper bag. Dad can barely hold on to Mary, who is wiggling until they reach the door. Once inside, Dad sets Mary down. Off she goes — a beeline to Miss Judy's class. She runs straight into Miss Judy's arms. Of course greetings only last a minute and then Mary is off again to check the toy area.

She picks up a doll, pokes it in the eyes a couple of times and then carries it with her until she sees a ball. She tries to pick up the ball while holding the doll and finds she cannot, so the doll is dropped and she now carries the ball over to Miss Judy.

"Ball," Mary says to Miss Judy.

"That's a big red ball, isn't it," says Miss Judy. "Let's show Daddy our red ball and say goodbye."

Mary runs to Dad and gives him the ball.

"Big ball," says Mary.

"What a pretty red ball," says Dad. "I have to go now Mary. Give me a hug goodbye."

Hug completed, Mary is off to investigate all the interesting things in Miss Judy's classroom.

TODDLERS

The name "toddler" refers to the unstable, lurching way in which toddlers fifteen to eighteen months begin walking (Mayesky, 1990). They cling to small furniture and launch themselves on unsteady journeys across the room to the next piece of support furniture. Toddlers use their new found mobility to explore the world of the day care center by touching, mouthing, and creating fantasy worlds with objects they find on the floor. Like the infant environment, the toddler daycare environment must also be safe and comfortable but include lots of objects toddlers can explore. At this stage of development, toddlers bring a rapidly growing collection of language accom-

plishments to the classroom. Here are some general guidelines that give you an idea of what toddlers can do with language and literacy (Morrow, 1997):

Language

1. Toddlers can produce one-word utterances
2. They begin to string words together ("allgone juice")
3. They love to play with sounds
4. They can distinguish between the concepts "you" and "me"
5. Toddlers can identify body parts
6. They enjoy responding to music
7. They are interested in playing with peers
8. They often say "no" emphatically

Literacy

1. Toddlers enjoy looking at books
2. They can turn the pages of a book
3. They can scribble
4. Toddlers begin categorizing objects in their play
5. They begin rote counting

The way you organize the environment of the day care area will have an impact on toddlers' language and literacy development. In the section that follows, we offer guidelines for a safe and nurturing setting for toddlers' new mobility and rapid learning curve.

TODDLER DAY CARE CLASSROOM SETTING

The day care setting for toddlers will be similar to the infant classroom. There should be plenty of bean-

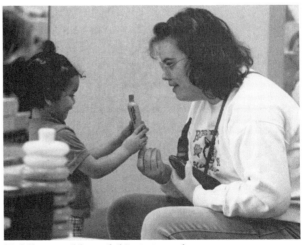

Toddlers need lots of objects to explore.

bag chairs, pillows, rugs, and places where children can stop to rest and explore objects, play with a cloth book, or simply catch their breath (Essa, 1996). A large open area with different play areas allows for various levels of play and learning. Toddlers mainly sit and play. Safe blocks, soft mattresses for jumping and tumbling, puzzles and labeled activity boxes encourage the wide-ranging exploration toddlers thrive on (Mayesky, 1990). The following list shows some of the furniture and equipment typically found in toddler indoor and outdoor environments:

Types of Furniture

Indoor:

Snacking and Lunchtime
  High chairs
  Feeding tables
  Small, low tables
  Child size chairs

Napping and Resting
  Rocking chair
  Cribs
  Arm chairs
  Beanbag chairs
  Rugs

Toileting
  Changing tables
  Storage shelves
  Free standing child's toilet
  Steps

Storage
  Cubbies
  Shelves for toys, books, and supplies
  Storage cabinets
  Bulletin boards

Toys
  Climbing equipment
  Push and pull toys
  Toddler wagons

Cribs, couches, rocking chairs, pillows, mattresses, and beanbags promote a warm nurturing area which creates a secure environment for resting. Opportunities for open-ended exploration, accessible materials and constant opportunities for grasping, reaching, pushing, and pulling should be made available. Mirrors add enjoyment to the infant environment.

As children begin to toddle around, they will be ready to explore the outdoors. An emphasis on safety

is important again in this area. The outdoor play area must be a safe area or you will be constantly following the children around. Time spent making your outdoor play area safe will save you time later.

Outdoor:

Climbing and Exploring Structures
  Steps
  Mini tunnels
  Small slides
  Cardboard boxes
  Block building areas
  Chimes
  Steering wheels
  Climbing area

Outdoor environments should be safe, secure, and exciting for children to explore. Soft ground for crawling, walking, running, and stepping up and down will help children expand their learning. There should be no high play structures or dangerous materials in the outdoor play area.

Noncrawling infants need an enclosed area that will encourage reaching, grasping and kicking. Infants enjoy baby sit-up swings and swinging cradles (Frost, 1992). The area should excite the infants' seeing and listening with wind chimes, prisms, mirrors, and natural sounds from the environment like breezes, birds, and crickets.

Infant and toddler environments are somewhat unique in how you schedule the essential activities of diapering, feeding, and nurturing children's development. The clear block schedules you will find in subsequent chapters of the book for older children really make little sense with infants and toddlers. In the section that follows we explore how you can manage scheduling in a flexible and workable way.

Mirrors add enjoyment to the environment.

Visit or think of an infant and toddler day care center you know and complete the following checklist. Exchange and discuss your responses with another class member

A Checklist for Infant and Toddler Environments

Directions: Place a check (✓) next to each statement that applies to the day care setting you observed.

Safety Concerns

_____ 1. Does the way the environment is arranged support the goals and objectives of the program?

_____ 2. Can children move freely in the environment and interact safely with each other, the teacher and the learning items available?

_____ 3. Can all children be seen at all times from all locations in the classroom?

_____ 4. Is the furniture appropriate for the physical size of infants and toddlers?

_____ 5. Does the environment accommodate infants and toddlers with special needs?

_____ 6. Is lighting adequate?

_____ 7. Are bathroom changing facilities located in a convenient area?

_____ 8. Are electric outlets covered when not being used and located in areas isolated from high interest areas?

_____ 9. Are the materials and supplies located in a convenient place so children have accessibility?

Learning Concerns

_____ 10. Are there visual clues for placement of materials and equipment?

_____ 11. Are storage containers labeled with objects, pictures, and photographs?

_____ 12. Are lots of child-centered books in evidence, including board and cloth books for infants and toddlers?

_____ 13. Are there opportunities for infants and toddlers to explore talking and listening while being diapered, fed, or getting ready for nap time?

_____ 14. Are infants and toddlers read to by the day care teachers and staff from books that excite their interest?

_____ 15. Are there enough staff to allow for one-on-one child-staff nurturing and teaching?

Scheduling in an Infant/Toddler Setting

It is hard to stick to a set schedule with infants and toddlers. An infant/toddler caregiver should be calm and flexible. There are many things that can disrupt a day with young children. A child's safety, happiness, and security is more important than whether you get to do an art activity. If all the children are changed and fed and down for their naps each day, give yourself a pat on the back. A weekly goal would be best for this age group.

If you are able to read to children in the course of your day, that will go a long way toward developing their love of stories and books. In fact, by handling books and playing with the idea of reading a story, even very young children are developing important ideas about what reading is for and its imaginative possibilities.

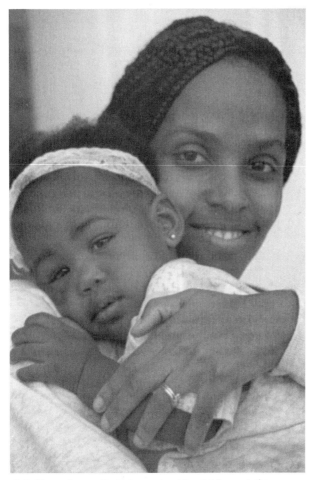

A feeling of security is important to children at this young age.

In the section that follows we introduce some good books to read and share with infants, as well as books they can play with on their own. Visit your public library and local bookstores for a wealth of additional books, tapes, puppets, and other language development materials.

BOOKS FOR INFANTS AND TODDLERS

Infants like visually stimulating books with faces, animals, trains, cars, and touch-and-feel qualities. Interactive, predictable, and pop-up books also interest very young children. They also like books with a rhythmical sound like Mother Goose. We have found that the following books capture infants' interest and attention and they will want you to read them repeatedly. Read them over-and-over as that provides the basis for good reading skills.

This listing includes a variety of book formats. Wordless picture books, pop-up books, scratch and sniff books, books with a few lines of print to read with related pictures, and board books that an infant or toddler can handle, all have a place in the day care environment. High quality infant and toddler books were published in the 1940's and 1950's, as well as more recent additions. So even older books you find at garage sales and used bookstores make great additions to your classroom collection. Most of the authors listed here have multiple books out in similar formats. Browsing your local bookstore and library will help track down the full range of their writings and it is simply a fun, relaxing way to spend some time. Most contemporary bookstores now feature cafe areas with coffee and tables to look over any books you might find. Or, enlisting the help of one of your older children in finding infant and toddler books can be a real boost to their self-esteem as "experts."

RESOURCES

Aliki. (1968). *Hush little baby: A folk lullaby.* New York: Simon & Schuster.

Arma, T. (1996). *Baby bugs.* New York: Grosset & Dunlop.

Asch, F. (1989). *Baby in the box.* New York: Holiday House.

Baer, G. (1996). *Thump, thump, rat-a-tat-tat.* New York: Harper Festival.

Butterworth, N. (1995). *All together now!* Boston, MA: Little, Brown.

Brown, R. (1985). *The big sneeze.* New York: William Morrow.

Carlstrom, N. W. (1994). *Tum-tum tickle.* New York: Macmillan.

Carlstrom, N. W. (1994). *Wiggle-jiggle jump-up.* New York: Macmillan.

Carter, A. (1991). *Dinner time.* New York: Price Stern Sloan.

Crews, D. (1978). *Freight train.* New York: Greenwillow.

Dubov, C. S. (1991). *Knock! And other sounds.* New York: William Morrow.

Ehlert, L. (1993). *Nuts to you.* Orlando, Florida: Harcourt, Brace, Jovanovich.

Falwell, C. (1991). *Nicky, 1 2 3.* New York: Clarion.

Goennel, H. (1995). *It's my world: What I eat.* New York: William Morrow.

Halpern, S. (1994). *Little Robin Redbreast: A Mother Goose rhyme.* New York: North-South.

Hill, E. (1991). *Spot in the garden.* New York: Putnam.

Hill, E. (1990). *Spot sleeps over.* New York: Putnam.

Hill, E. (1985). *Spot at play.* New York: Putnam.

Hill, E. (1980). *Where's Spot?* New York: Putnam.

Hoban, T. (1985). *A children's zoo.* New York: William Morrow.

Hoban, T. (1979). *One little kitten.* New York: Greenwillow.

Hutchins, P. (1972). *Goodnight owl!* New York: Macmillan.

Kunhardt, D. (1984). *Pat the bunny.* Racine, WI: Western Publishing Co.

MacDonald, A., & Roffey, M. (1994). *Let's pretend.* London: Walker.

Martin, B. (1989). *Chicka chika boom boom.* New York: Simon & Schuster.

Martin, B. (1983). *Brown bear, brown bear, what do you see?* New York: Holt.

Two-year-olds love books.

Miller, M. (1996). *Family time.* New York: Simon & Schuster.

Miller, M. (1994). *Guess who?* New York: Greenwillow.

Morris, A. (1990). *This little baby's bedtime.* New York: Orchard.

Oxenbury, H. (1987). *All fall down.* New York: Macmillan.

Pandell, K. (1994). *I love you, sun, I love you moon.* New York: Putnam.

Peppe, R. (1996). *The magic toy box.* Cambridge, MA: Candlewick Press.

Pienkowski, J. (1993). *ABC dinosaurs.* New York: Dutton.

Risom, O. (1970). *I am a puppy.* New York: Golden Press.

Tafuri, N. (1988). *Two new sneakers.* Albany, New York: Greenwillow.

Tafuri, N. (1987). *Do not disturb.* New York: Greenwillow.

Williams, S. (1990). *I went walking.* San Diego, CA: Harcourt Brace.

Zokeisha. *Things I like to play with.* New York: Simon and Schuster.

In addition to your local librarian, bookstores and used bookstores, garage sales, friends, publisher catalogs, and newsletters, here are some additional resources you can use to find good books for infants and toddlers.

Additional Resources for Finding Books

A number of textbooks on children's literature include recommended listings for infants and toddlers. Most contemporary children's literature texts now come with diskettes that list books and are easy to search by categories such as topics or age groups.

Jacobs, J. S., & Tunnel, M. O. (1996). *Children's literature briefly.* Englewood Cliffs, NJ: Merrill.

Norton, D. (1995). *Through the eyes of a child* (4th ed.). Englewood Cliffs, NJ: Prentice-Hall.

Books on literacy in early childhood also offer excellent lists of books including those appropriate for infants and toddlers. For example:

Morrow, L. M. (1997). *Literacy development in the early years: Helping children read and write* (3rd ed.). Boston: Allyn and Bacon.

Newsletters from publishers and bookstores also review current books, feature author autograph sessions, and include book order forms. On the West Coast, we enjoy The White Rabbit Children's Books (bookstore) regular newsletters and book reviews, often organized by holiday themes. Each review includes illustrations and an indication of the appropriate ages for the book. You can write to the following address to get their newsletter:

The While Rabbit Children's Books
7755 Girard Ave.
La Jolla, CA 92037
Phone: 1-800-920-9000 or (619) 454-3518

In addition to your work in the classroom, you will need to keep in regular contact with infant and toddler parents. The pace of your regular day care day may prevent the level of contact and information sharing with parents you might like. A monthly parent newsletter can go along way toward building and maintaining bridges to literacy and healthy child development for infants and toddlers. Below is a sample monthly parent letter:

SAMPLE

Infant and Toddler Parent Letter

In May we will be concentrating on our sense of touch as well as continuing to work on body awareness. We will be giving the children lots of different things to touch and feel. I have many different surfaces to put on the floor for the infants to roll around on and the toddlers to walk and jump on. We will be bringing out some new toys with interesting feelings and textures.

My goals for the month are:

April 28 to May 5 - Soft and hard toys
May 6th to 12th - Scratchy and smooth
May 13 to 20 - Warm and cold
May 21 to 28 - Wet and dry

Parent Tip: Be aware of the different feelings and textures your child is experiencing in his everyday life. Talk with him about it. When you are changing his diaper you might comment on how cold and wet the diaper wipe is, or how soft his shirt is.

Other News: Jordan will be one year old May 17th. Happy Birthday!

Park Day will be on May 23rd. We need parent volunteers.

Reminder: Safety check your home for safety hazards like exposed electrical outlets.

Sincerely,
Miss Thomas

As toddlers approach their second birthdays, they will be more interested in such activities as block play, simple puzzles, and books. They will also dress up and play with house toys like play dishes. Much of a toddler's time will be spent moving around the room, pushing and pulling toys, and dragging dolls and blankets. These toys will be left wherever the child lost interest in them.

Additional Teacher Resources

Activities:

Mayesky, M. E. (1990). *Creative activities for infants, toddlers, and twos.* Chicago, IL: Fearon.

Journals and Newsletters:

Day Care and Early Education
Human Sciences Press
233 Spring St.
New York, NY 10013

Day Care U. S. A. Newsletter
Day Care Information Service
1300 Rockville Pike, #1100
Rockville, MD 20852

Early Childhood Teacher
730 Broadway
New York, NY 10003

Nanny Times
135 Sylvan St.
Rutherford, NJ 07070

Young Children
National Association for the Education of Young Children
1834 Connecticut Ave. NW
Washington, DC 20009-5786

REFERENCES

Essa, E. (1996). *Introduction to early childhood education* (2nd ed.). New York: Delmar.

Frost, J. (1992). *Play and playscapes.* Albany, NY: Delmar.

Howes, C., & Hamilton, C. E. (1993). Child care for young children. In B. Spodek (Ed.), *Handbook of research on the education of young children.* New York: Macmillan.

Kamerman, S. B., & Kahn, A. J. (1995). *Starting right: How America neglects its youngest children and what we can do about it.* New York: Oxford University Press.

Mayesky, M. E. (1990). *Creative activities for infants, toddlers, and twos.* Chicago, IL: Fearon.

Morrow, L. M. (1997). *Literacy development in the early years: Helping children read and write* (3rd ed.). Boston, MA: Allyn and Bacon.

CHAPTER 3

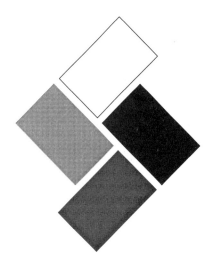

Developing Effective Preschool Environments

Before she went to preschool, Felicia often went with her mother to complete errands around town. The route to the grocery store is lined with a number of fast food chains. Now at age three, Felicia sits in her car seat and supplies her mother with a running travelogue of establishments along the way. "'At's McDonald's. 'At's Tucky Fried. 'At's Pizza, and Dunkin Donuts."

Inside the supermarket, Felicia sits in the grocery cart and continues her travelogue up and down the aisles. "'At's Pop Tarts. 'At's Cheerios. 'At's Oreos. 'At's Coke." Sometimes her mother hands her articles and asks, "What does that say?" pointing to the product name. At other times, Felicia reverses the role and asks her mother what various labels "say."

Through her journey to the grocery store with its print rich array of signs, products, and bright lights, Felicia is learning the functions of print in a natural way. Preschool environments that build on Felicia's early encounters with print will make her voyage a smooth one.

Nixon at age four spends several short periods each day in dialogue with his stuffed animal collection reading books. He sorts the books into piles on the floor, naming each one in turn and placing them in stacks according to some system of categorizing known only to Nixon. After carefully sorting, he then asks his stuffed animals which book they would like to hear.

"Oh, I don't think you want to read that one," he will say, if he is in the mood for a longer session. "I know one you want to hear. It's my best book. It says, *Brown Bear, Brown Bear, What do You See?*" (Martin & Carle, 1983).

Then Nixon selects one stuffed animal, a bear, and proceeds to read the book page by page. He has heard his preschool teacher read the story so often that he now has it memorized. Sometimes, he will inadvertently skip a page or two and say, "Oh, we skipped something! I better go back because you want to hear that part." If he grows tired, he will say, "Oh, you don't want to hear about that. This page sounds better."

Both Felicia and Nixon bring a sense of print to the preschool environment. In addition to play reading, they both color and draw pictures of the world around them. This combination of print awareness and artistic response to the world around them offers a natural foundation for creating effective preschool environments.

One of the best ways to engage preschool children in print rich literacy experiences is to create literacy enriched play centers. Literacy enriched play centers foster children's natural curiosity and language development (Rybczynski & Troy, 1995). Indeed, children are avid enthusiasts and supporters of literacy enriched play centers.

Literacy enriched play centers foster children's language development.

PRESCHOOL CHILDREN'S VIEWS

When children are asked to recall activities at preschool, they relate to learning centers that are usually their favorites. For example, Rachel, who was almost five said: "I like to play at the Play Dough Center." Nick, at three and a half said, "I like the Dinosaur Center. And, Morgan, also three and a half said, "I like the Housekeeping Center."

Each of these children found themselves in preschool settings that encouraged creativity and play as a bridge to literacy. They were read to at home and they had particular book preferences. For example, Nick said, "My mom and sister read to me all the time. I like books about dolphins."

The flow of activities in a preschool day encourages or restricts children's enthusiasm for learning through play. For example, the following schedule is fairly typical and works well with an activity-based preschool structure.

Children relate to their favorite learning center.

SCHEDULE

8:00	Arrival time
8:00	Free choice — Centers
9:00	Circle time
9:30	Outside time
10:00	Bathroom & wash hands
10:15	Snack
10:30	Free choice — Project (art, cooking, science centers)
11:15	Bathroom & wash-up for lunch
11:30	Lunch
11:45	Read stories while children finish lunch
12:00	Nap & Teacher preparation time
1:30	Activity — independent for children waking-up
2:00	Wake-up & wash up
2:30	Snack
2:45	Outside play
3:30	Do circle time review, center time, or art activity and free choice
4:00	Children start to be picked-up

EXPANDING PRESCHOOL ENVIRONMENTS FOR LITERACY

Many preschool teachers begin working with young children out of an interest in their own families. Michelle teaches three-year-olds because it allows her greater time to be with her young son.

In her teaching, Michelle builds on children's natural curiosity about their names to help them learn alphabet letters. They color letters, glue beans on letters, and play games. They put sand in trays and write the letters of their names. Michelle starts small with an emphasis on letter recognition of the first letter in each child's name. One of the best ways for children to learn to recognize letters and their meaning is through recognizing their own and other children's names. At circle time, the teacher calls roll by showing each child's name card. The children learn how to spell their names in this way.

Nancy, another preschool teacher of two and three year olds, relates the alphabet to the names of the various children in the room, and other familiar words.

For example, A is for Anthony, B is for Brittany, and F is for fun, because no one in her class has a name beginning with F. In addition, when children create their own pictures in the art center, they dictate to Ms. Nancy what they want to call it. One child, Brandon, scribbled a picture and said, "I made a letter D." Brandon's mom can read what Brandon dictated and Ms. Nancy wrote when he takes his picture home. Brandon is beginning to connect the squiggles on his picture with talk, a first step to reading.

You can ask children to "hold up your name if you are here today" with a card displaying a child's name. They also have a natural interest in how other children's names are made. Or, as you develop centers, you can ask, "Who is going to the housekeeping center?" Children hold up their name cards to indicate interest.

Joni teaches four and five year olds. She developed a large classroom library of wordless picture books like Nina Crew's (1995), *One Hot Summer Day*, and Eric Carle's (1996), *Little Cloud*. It is important to "read" these picture books by making up a story as you go that engages children's interest.

You can make up your own words to a story if you find that children are bored by the material. Similarly, if you decide to read your all time favorite book and children appear not to share this same level of enthusiasm for the story, return to a book they like. Even if you have your *If You Give a Mouse a Cookie* (Numeroff, 1985) tee shirt on and the big book version of this story, preschool children may not be familiar with the book and may tune you out on an initial reading. Try to resist the urge to drag them bodily through your cherished book that day.

In her classroom, Joni also used predictable books like Robert Kalan's (1981), *Jump, Frog, Jump*. Joni distributes the book list for her room to parents. She encourages parents to read to their children at home by asking children to retell stories they listened to the night before and placing a sticker on a wall chart in the room each day they recount a story. Joni has a Listening Center in her room where children can follow along in a book with a corresponding tape. These "talking books" help children develop a strong interest in stories and a sense of how a story is created (Walker, 1996).

Selecting books from the children's library center in the classroom, rather than a book only the teacher has, is important because it shows that these books are great, too. Equally important is reading a book children prefer repeatedly rather than bouncing around from book-to-book. Children often imitate book reading after listening repeatedly to a story they like. This pretend reading sets the stage for letter and word recognition, dictating stories, and story reading in kindergarten. We know a preschool teacher who

Children often imitate book reading after listening repeatedly to a story they like.

read *Jump, Frog, Jump* (Kalan, 1981) often to children. Once they had the drift of this predictable book, they could "read" it as she displayed each page and its accompanying pictures. The teacher taped children doing a choral reading of the story and placed this tape in the listening center. Children were thrilled to hear themselves reading a favorite story. Their parents could also listen to their reading of the story.

You can locate children's books at garage sales and library sales. In addition, children can bring in favorite books to share for the week. You may want to provide parents with a list of needed books for the preschool. These suggested books can become a "birthday present" children give to the book center reading area of the school.

Judy, another preschool teacher, organizes her preschool class of four and five year olds around learning centers. Her centers are based on weekly themes related to bugs, the circus, growing plants, colors, shapes, holidays, and seasons. Centers should be labeled. If a weekly theme focuses on "bugs," the word BUGS should be prominently displayed at the center along with insect picture clues to the word. Each center can accommodate a certain number of children at a time. This number, along with picture clues of three stick figures or other symbols indicating the number

able to use the center at any one time, is posted above each center. Children learn to count, partially by paying attention to these numbers and symbols, especially when too many children cluster at one center.

Judy feels strongly that you should use authentic or "real" items in the centers. If children are learning about growing beans, plant real seeds to observe their growth cycle. Judy stocks her room with books linked to the weekly theme by consulting with the librarian at the local public library. She also searches the public library database for books on the weekly theme using the computer in the library or from her home to link into the library collections.

Judy believes that learning should be fun because preschoolers learn through play. Children need hugs and praise. They need to be stimulated and encouraged. Judy has no use for little desks where three to five-year-olds do worksheets all day. Her feeling is that when an activity becomes boring or is of no interest, you should put it away and try it when the children may enjoy it.

Judy manages her classroom using a combination of traffic flow routines children learn in order to play in the centers. They sing transition songs to move from playtime to circle time. For example, Judy uses nursery rhymes and well-known songs to make-up transition songs. She uses the patterns from "Here We Go Round the Mulberry Bush" to have children sing the transition song "Circle Time."

Let's all get ready for circle time, circle time, circle time
Let's all get ready for circle time
Come and sit down

When it is time to clean up after centers or other play times, you can use familiar rhythms from "Barney" or other television shows children know to

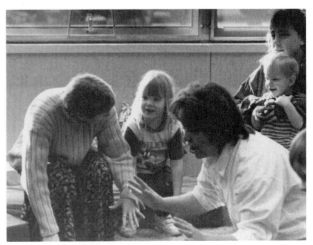

Learning should be fun!

make this transition fun. For example, the following song helps children switch gears from play to clean up:

> It's clean-up time in the classroom now
> It's time for girls and boys
> To stop what they are doing now
> And put away their toys

Thus, given the many songs children know from television, radio, and advertisements, you can easily add words to familiar rhythms so that transitions from one activity to the next are fun. In addition, you can display the songs, engage children in dictating more rhyming verses, and use music to further build their awareness that print is "talk written down."

ORGANIZING THE CLASSROOM ENVIRONMENT

Constructing a print rich classroom environment requires some planning, especially if your space was not originally designed as a preschool, which is often the case. Preschools can be successful in a variety of adapted buildings ranging from church classrooms to refurbished houses. Although general guidelines exist suggesting minimal square footage-per-child, (usually in the range of 35 to 100 square feet in a large rectangular shaped room), the important point is that *children should not be crowded into a space* (Essa, 1996).

Preschool children need to be able to explore their environment and make free choices about center activities, books, and play. Indeed, for cognitive and language growth, they need many opportunities to experiment with blocks, art, drama, science, music, and other areas where they interact with peers and co-construct knowledge (Vygotsky, 1962). How you arrange the classroom will encourage or limit learning. Naturally, safety is an issue as you construct a learner-centered environment.

To get started, you should draw a sketch of your classroom. Figure 3.1 shows a preschool classroom with centers that change periodically to encourage variety and exploration. In the section that follows, we help you construct a preschool classroom and suggest how it is managed by the teacher and a teacher assistant. We then describe various centers and reading materials that might be included in a preschool classroom. You may have to combine various centers because of available space.

The goal of this classroom is to make learning fun and enrich children's experiences with print in its many forms and functions.

Take a moment to take a tour through the various centers and materials listed on Figure 3.1.

Children need to operate the centers themselves. For example, if they play with a toy, they return it to its storage shelf when they are done. This frees you to roam the room and work with children whenever they need your help.

Limiting the number of children who can work in a center to a reasonable number is crucial. You can use a system of stop and go, red and green lights, or tags students pick up as they begin working in a particular center. When they are done working in a center, they return the tag to a hanger. This is also a good place to include words like "stop" and "go," along with the children's names. A simple sign with a number and stick figures indicating the number for each center can also work. By limiting the number of children in a center you can reduce crowding and encourage them to try a variety of centers.

You should keep all the shelving in the room at a level where you can see children in the various centers from anyplace in the room when you are standing.

It is also important to understand that while the centers in Figure 3.1 have established names and places in the room, their content can change weekly or monthly depending on themes being explored. Changing center content stimulates children's interest and learning. Avoid putting out too much for children to play with at any one time. They will enjoy the variety and you will keep clean up time to a manageable level.

Let us tour the actual centers in our classroom to get a better picture of how you might set-up your classroom.

THE BOOK CENTER

The book center should have open access, but also include an area separated by tables and shelves where quiet reading can occur. It is also important to organize other quiet centers adjacent to the book center rather than placing the more active and noisy blocks and dramatic play centers close to the book center.

The book center needs an open area for relaxing on the floor. A comfortable carpet and pillows or beanbags make this an attractive place to explore print. A nearby shelf should be arranged so children can easily see the cover of books they might want to look at. The bulletin board can feature eye catching colored posters and interactive packets with matching alphabet, words, and pictures. Figure 3.2 illustrates one form of interactive bulletin board you can create.

This interactive bulletin board is made so you can easily change the concept taught. On the figure, the packets labeled "slots" and the boxes remain on the board (using staples or other anchors to attach them).

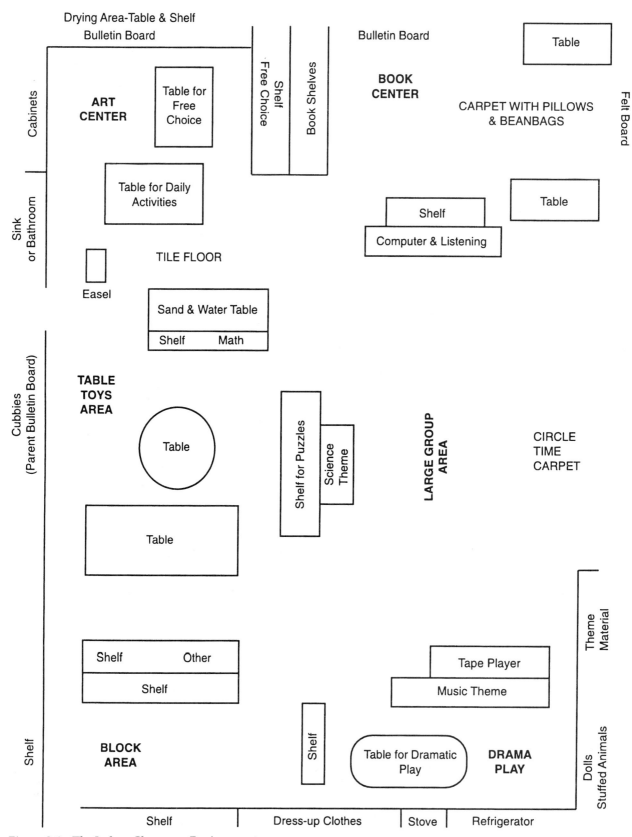

Figure 3.1. The Indoor Classroom Environment

The book center needs an open area for relaxing on the floor.

The ABC's can be changed to numbers, colors. Even things like rocks, plants, and animals.

In Figure 3.2, the slots may hold cards with alphabet letters, colors, numbers, and so on, that children take from the large box at the bottom of the figure. Some of these pictures will match the pictures stapled to the boards corresponding to the matching alphabet letters, and others will not match. For example, children can decide where the "apple, ant, block, banana, caterpillar, and car" should go. The boxes below the slots are attached to the wall and contain the item children match to the letters, colors, and so on.

A felt board is a valuable addition to the book center so those children can create their own stories. You can provide felt pieces showing animals, cars, houses, and other concrete objects likely to be found in the picture and predictable books children explore in the center. Felt pieces of characters can be used to "tell" the story of a specific book you are currently reading

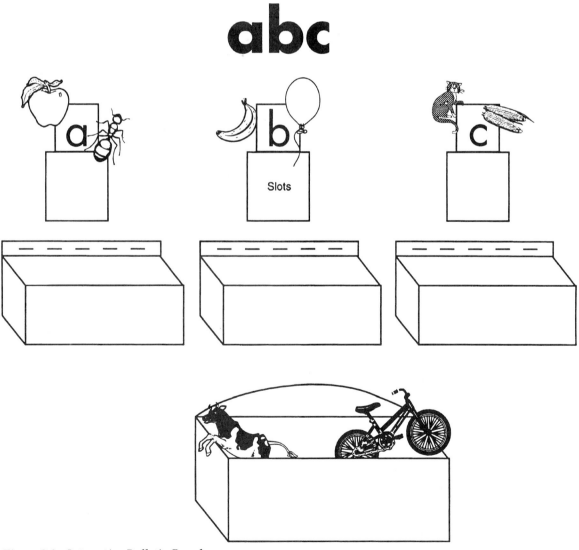

Figure 3.2. Interactive Bulletin Board

Floor plan for Barnyard Kids Preschool indoor learning environment. (Designed by Sybil Lee Lane)

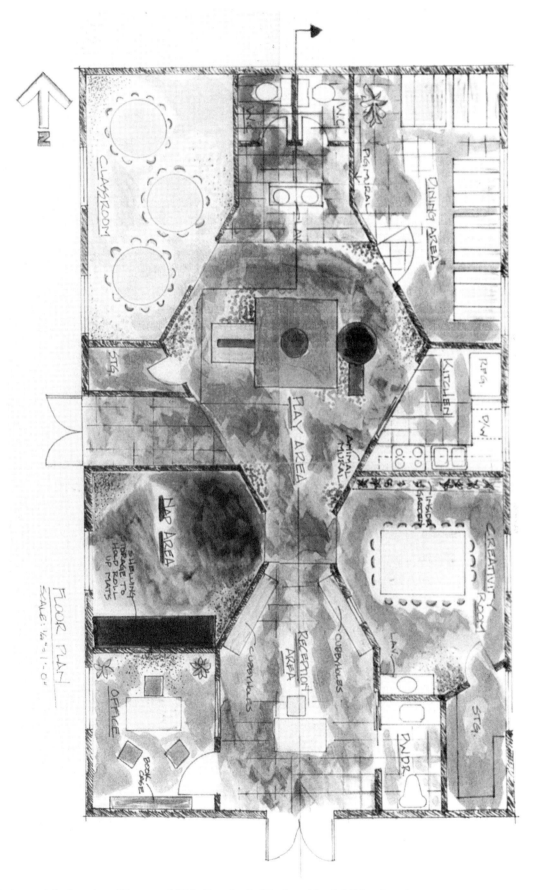

Renderings of the interior of Barnyard Kids Preschool. (Designed by Sybil Lee Lane)

to them. Figure 3.3 shows a felt board with farm animal figures.

The picture at the top of the figure is one children created using the farm animal felt pieces at the bottom of the figure. Children can create pictures based on a story you read to them during story time, or they may make up their own story using the felt board. Encourage children to create picture stories after a song is sung, too.

The felt board can be free standing or attached to the wall like a bulletin board with a box or tray on the floor containing felt pieces and figures.

Children want to imitate your circle time reading. They can use your reading chair or a small table and chairs where they can sit and read to their friends. Children also like to imitate Mommy, Daddy, brothers and sisters or other relatives by reading to others. An additional shelf or basket can contain puppets and stuffed animals. These can also be used as "babies" to be read to or characters in a made-up story. You can have a table or shelf where alphabet books, word games, and other toys related to books are easily found and played with in the book center. Paper and pencils, as well as washable ink markers come in handy when children want to make their own books using non-messy materials in the book center.

You may want to have a shelf or area in the book center to hold books about a theme you are introducing that week. If children were exploring the world of dinosaurs, then this particular section of the book center would feature books about dinosaurs. It is important to have a mix of permanent books children see and explore repeatedly, and a floating collection of books that are about a particular theme.

If you are limited in overall classroom space, the book center can double as a circle time area as the shelf spaces can be shared and changed. All the shelves should be labeled. For example: BOOKS, BOOK TOYS, GAMES, and so on.

What books might be good to have in the book center? At the end of the chapter, we list some of our favorites. The best strategy is to talk with other preschool teachers, staff, parents, and librarians and also be on the lookout for good children's books recommended in professional resources and journals in early childhood, library, English, and reading; and literacy and early childhood web sites. Attending workshops or conferences where publishers exhibit books will also give you access to new books. Ask to have your name added to publishers' mailing lists as you browse the exhibits. Pay careful attention to the age of your children. Check for local children's bookstores that offer workshops and meet-the-author sessions for children, parents, and teachers. A two-year-old requires different books than a four-year-old.

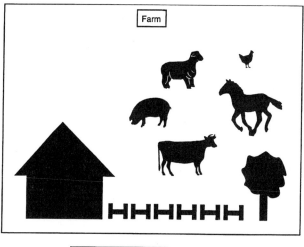

Figure 3.3. Farm Animal Felt Board

THE ART CENTER

Like the book center, the art center is a fairly quiet area but it needs to be separated from the rest of the classroom because it can be "messy." There should be a sink in the area if possible, or have the area located next to a bathroom so you can use the sink there. Because this is a "messy" area, it will require lots of teacher direction at first to teach children to clean up and put away supplies. Start slowly with a few materials that require minimal clean up and show the children how you want the area cleaned up and where to store materials.

You can think about the art center as having both "free choice" materials and activities and "teacher assisted" activities. The free choice area features art materials available for the children to use without your supervision and or direction. Paper, crayons, scissors, glue sticks, scrap paper, colored pens and pencils form a basic collection of materials. These materials should be available all the time and changed periodically to encourage children to experiment with new materials. Additionally, you need a storage cabinet in the area for easy teacher access to art materials for the daily activities.

Teacher assisted art can build on the theme of the week with a daily art activity using play dough, paints, crayons, glue, and so on. It is important to note that this does not have to be a teacher directed activity, you can give some directions and then help as needed. Teacher directed art, however, usually involves "messy" art with paint, glue, or special theme related art and instruction. This is particularly true with the introduction of a new activity with new materials. The art center may double as an area for cooking activities since it usually has a sink and surfaces for mixing recipe ingredients.

The art center needs to have a large table or shelf to serve as a drying surface where children can put their artwork to dry. A clothesline with clothespins creates a great drying area, too. You can write children's names on wooden clothespins. If possible, each child should have a cubby in this center. Children should become familiar with placing their own work in the cubbies or on the table to dry.

An easel may be useful when you or the teacher assistant are supervising children's painting. During free choice times, the easel can contain chalk, markers, crayons, and other materials less messy than paint. Taping newspapers or a large sheet of plastic drop cloth or cardboard makes clean up easier too.

The water table can be changed with food coloring or soap. It should also be used for texture play. You can experiment with sand, flour, beans, rice, goop, or even ice, shaving cream, or Jell-O. Children can experiment with scribbling, drawing, or simply talking about the different textures they feel.

Children's art should be displayed prominently on the walls and bulletin boards of the art center, as well as throughout the rest of the classroom. These displays can change as themes shift over the weeks and months. Many children want to take all their creations home. Ask them for a picture for the classroom wall but be sure they know they can take their displayed art home when they want to. They will not mind displaying it in the classroom art gallery. Children should create a name for the art gallery area of their classroom.

Children's pictures provide a vehicle to introduce reading through dictation stories. Ask children to tell you about their pictures and write what they say. For example, Nathan might identify his scribbles as a racing car going really fast. Write down his words on the scribble picture he made. Nathan and his parents can "read" them later on.

TABLE TOYS CENTER

The table toy center is a place where children can play and explore with a lot of free choice. The center should have shelves that contain a variety of manipulative toys such as puzzles, small blocks, stringing beads, and games. This is a good center in which to introduce children to math activities through manipulatives including matching, sorting, and counting. Be careful not to exhaust all your activities at one time in this center. Alternate manipulatives and activities weekly.

Children's cubbies can be located here because this is an easy area for parents to get children involved in table activities that distract them, easing the transition from home to preschool for both children and parents. Each child should have a cubby area for clothes, jacket, artwork and so on. Cubbies can be labeled with children's names to further make the print-environment link. Children may bring photographs of themselves to identify cubbies.

The cubby area is an ideal place to locate a parent bulletin board for announcements, parenting ideas, and fun activities to do with children. You also can put a parent mailbox here. The mailbox can be a small letter size box or folder with each parent's name where you leave preschool information, notes, and so on. As parents check their child's cubby, they will remember to check their mailboxes too.

A bulletin board can be placed in this center for daily or weekly notes about the week's activity: "We made play dough today. We're going to the zoo to-

The water table can be used to experiment with sand and other textures.

morrow." These can be daily news announcements that children dictate to you for parent display on the daily activity bulletin board. They can also be funny things that happened. Instant photos or brief announcements of something special that happened that day are great to display in this area, too. Photos may relate to the current theme being explored and children can illustrate them in the art center. A school scrapbook that features photos and artwork of special projects children completed may be displayed in this area for parents and classroom visitors.

LARGE GROUP AREA

The large group area is often part of a center like the book center or block area, wherever you have space. In Figure 3.1 (see page 26), we show the large group area adjacent to the art center.

Circle time usually occurs in the large group area. It should be a fun time to encourage language. You can create short activities to grab children's attention through songs or finger plays. Circle time can keep one group of children occupied and engaged while another group cleans up after art or play activities in another center. Circle time also makes taking attendance easier when you involve the whole class in a single activity. Children love to hear their names called while they learn their classmates' names. Circle time can lead into a puppet show, game, lesson, or music related to the theme you are working with that week. Children thrive on repetition and circle time is a good point to tie-together concepts and activities from children's exploration of the centers. Children have short attention spans and need to be "involved" in

Circle time is a great time to read aloud to children.

circle time. For example, adding expressive movement to your reading of a story gets children into the flow and mood of a predictable book.

Circle time also offers a great opportunity to read aloud to children from predictable books. However, if they seem bored with the book you are reading do not hesitate to drop it and return to books they genuinely enjoy. Sometimes this is painful if you have brought your favorite story or a new book you found in the library, but your audience of preschoolers may not share your enthusiasm for a particular book.

The Large Group Area (music, science, computer, and listening) also contains theme tables. These tables can be used interchangeably as they are needed for thematic units or other activities.

You can see in Figure 3.2 that the organization of the room flows from the relatively quiet areas of the book center and art center to the more active, noisy table toy and large group sections of the room. The next two areas are the noisiest.

THE BLOCK CENTER

The block center encourages children to create and explore interesting shapes, designs, and structures that become places for imaginative play. Block centers foster oral language development, creativity, and math skills. The block area should be carpeted to keep the noise down.

This center should have a collection of large blocks including wood blocks, cardboard blocks and boxes, waffle type blocks and plastic blocks. You should change the blocks in this center periodically to maintain children's interest and provide different building materials for their exploration. In addition to blocks for building structures, this center may have small and large toy cars. These toys should change periodically along with a collection of miniature people and animals, stuffed animals, and puppets. These props help children create their own plays.

DRAMATIC PLAY CENTER

The dramatic play center should contain a table and chairs, along with a collection of household materials including a stove, refrigerator, dishes, pots and pans, and utensils. You should also stock this center with dolls, stuffed animals, puppets, dress-up clothes, play telephone with paper and pencil for messages, and anything else related to dramatic play. You can obtain many of these items through parent help and donations. Label areas so that children see the words connected to their activities: TABLE, STOVE, TELE-PHONE, and so on.

The dramatic play center is a great place to launch themes related to daily life. For example, you can turn your dramatic play center into a pet shop, beauty parlor, restaurant, birthday party, grocery store, or hospital. The list of possible themes is endless and often suggested by children's interests.

These stable centers form the core of the preschool room's indoor environment. Like a kitchen where the daily meals vary, the choices of what you and the children do weekly in the centers is not limited. We will be looking at some of the themes you may want to introduce, along with how to use the outdoor preschool environment you organize. The benefits of play centers and literacy enriched play centers are many and we will discuss them next.

THE ROLE OF PLAY CENTERS

Children's experiences are the basis for storytelling that organizes these experiences. Preschool children at first use drawing to support storytelling and represent their thoughts. They often label their drawings with letters and scribbles that explain their drawings (Britsch, 1993). In addition to circle time, being read to, transition songs, and whole group literacy activities, preschool children need time to construct an understanding of reading and writing in their lives. Play centers create interest, social interaction, and an exciting place for drawing, writing, and talking about the world.

LITERACY-ENRICHED PLAY CENTERS

Literacy-enriched play centers are usually based on a theme brainstormed with children (Rybczynski & Troy, 1995). Themes that children typically express interest in include: bugs, dinosaurs, post office, library, cars, animals, grocery store, restaurants, and so on. A literacy-enriched center fosters exploration of written language through marking, scribbling, letter recognition, copying words, invented and standard spelling, and simply noticing how print functions to make things happen. A good center is child initiated, naturally motivating, hands-on, and appropriate for the developmental age of a preschooler (Rybczynski & Troy, 1995).

For example, a grocery store center may include signs, coupons, checkbooks, cereal boxes, cans, and other items that involve print as a medium of organization. The kinds of language used in this center are linked to play. For example, a real grocery store is a necessary and important place where print plays an important role. Children can create their own store in your classroom. They can "pretend" to shop, buy and

The dramatic play center includes items like a stove and refrigerator.

sell goods, depending on their role in the imaginary store.

A grocery store play center should include realistic items that encourage literacy play. These might include: a typewriter, boxes of cereal, cans, signs that say "open" and "closed," a desk, store signs donated by a real grocery store, ads, cash register, coupons, inventories, play money, purses, pads, and paper.

SKETCHING A PRESCHOOL YOU KNOW

As you think about preschools where you have observed or worked, are they language rich? In the space on the next page, can you sketch how the environment is organized? To what extent does it look like the school we described in Figure 3.1? How would you change the school you drew? Represent these changes in a contrasting color on your drawing. You may want to do your sketch using a drawing software package.

A Preschool I Know

The outdoor environment is more important than simply a place for large motor activities and letting off steam when you move to a thematic and language enriched curriculum. It can become a place for observation and discussion that links classroom themes to the six centers in Figure 3.1.

THE OUTDOOR ENVIRONMENT

As the children in your classroom explore a variety of themes, the natural world of the outdoors can support this learning (Essa, 1996). Observations and discussion of insects, plants, weather, and animal care are all possibilities as part of theme exploration.

Children cannot run, climb, or yell while indoors. The outdoor playground should be a place where they can exercise their bodies and lungs. It should have lots of open space for active play and something safe to climb on. A jungle gym built over a rubber mat or in a sandy area is best. Concrete playgrounds should be avoided. There also should be some shaded area for wet or hot days.

Swings and slides, a sandbox, water table, bicycles, tables, and chairs, and a playhouse can be added, depending on your budget and space available. They provide additional opportunities for concrete and imaginative play, and language. In addition to those areas that can be made with parent and volunteer help, there are many commercial things available for outdoor playgrounds.

Outdoor discussions can support weekly themes you and the children are exploring. For example, if "how plants grow" is a theme under consideration, children can plant a garden to tend. They can draw their garden, read about vegetables and related stories, and sing a song about it.

They can go on a nature walk outdoors to collect leaves, cones, and other materials. These objects can form the basis for art, reading, and songs. For example, children can make-up a song like the one that follows and you can tape record it. Later on, they can create illustrations for the song and take copies home to share with their families.

 *We went on a nature hike
And this is what we found*

(The teacher points to each child to make up a line of the song with what they found)

I found a pine cone brown and round (and so on)

Children can collect and study small insects. Simple children's reference books support each of these topics and the outdoors is a great place to start this exploration.

Even in cold weather climates, the outdoors, seen through the classroom windows, can be a great place

An outdoor playground should have something safe to climb on.

for observation of clouds and weather patterns. Countless children's books support and extend children's observations. In the section that follows, we demonstrate how to develop weekly themes such as ants, using resources in the classroom and outdoors to extend children's language learning.

A WEEK-LONG THEME ON ANTS

A thematic unit focuses children's learning activities on a central topic (Allen & Piersma, 1995). Preschool children can explore a topic through circle time, learning center hands-on activities, and listening to children's literature that illuminates the topic through picture books, stories, informational books, poetry, drama, and music. Preschool children's questions and interests offer a great launching pad for week-long thematic units. In this section, we illustrate one teacher's use of circle time sharing to create a week-long unit on ants. Although there are a number of books designed to help you in planning units, we offer a simple planning model of how preschool teachers can plan a unit in the brief time they have to develop activities and collect materials for various centers. Of course, the more units you create, the easier it is to adapt materials and construct new units. Capturing and holding young children's interest and shifting attention spans is a challenge. In the first activity that fits a week-long timeline for a unit, the teacher capitalizes on children's already high interest in ants.

Ants

Day 1. Introducing the Unit

It is nine o'clock in Susan's preschool. Children have arrived and they are sharing items in the morning circle time. Nathan brought in an ant farm his grandparents gave him for his birthday. He is really excited about it and the other children also enjoy watching the ants scurry through the tunnels of their home, carrying bits of food.

Susan knows there are some ant books in the book center, including Chris Van Allsburg's (1988) *Two bad ants*. Her assistant teacher, Dan, goes over to the center and gets the book. Susan asks the children, "Would you like to learn more about ants this week?" They all say, "yes!"

She starts by reading *Two bad ants* aloud. It is the story of a group of worker ants trying to find tasty sugar crystals for their queen. Two of the ants cannot resist staying behind to eat lots of the sugar crystals while their fellow ants return home. The "two bad ants" get into a series of problems and they barely

escape disaster. The story is a great launching pad for a themed unit on ants.

Susan also introduces children to the well known counting song, "The ants go marching" (Beall, 1996). Susan plays the notes on the piano and they sing:

 The ants go marching one by one, Hur-rah,-Hur-rah
The ants go marching one by one, Hur-rah, Hur-rah
The ants go marching one by one,
The little one stops to suck his thumb
And they all go marching down to the ground
To get out of the rain, BOOM! BOOM! BOOM!

Other verses change line 4 to:

 Two.....tie his shoe
Three.....climb a tree
Four.....shut the door
Five.....take a dive
Six.....pick up sticks
Seven.....pray to heaven
Eight.....shut the gate
Nine.....check the time
Ten.....say, "THE END"

During the part of the 9:00 to 10:00 o'clock morning circle time, when children are getting "antsy," Susan asks if they want to go outside and look for ants. They take plastic jars and head outdoors to hunt for ants.

Day 2. What Are Ants?

Susan and Dan use a simple unit plan to build children's interests in a short period of time. A visit to the library for ant books and cutting out some "ant shapes" prepare them for the week ahead. After yesterday's circle time, Susan and Dan plotted extension activities for the rest of the week using a daily calendar.

During circle time on the second day, Susan shared with the children selected parts of the informational book, *Ant cities* (Dorros, 1987), a book that shows how ants make their tunnels and collect food. She then showed them photos that illustrate the parts of an ant's body in the book *Ants* (Overbeck, 1982). Both books are available in public libraries and she tracked them down with her home computer using her internet connection to search for the topic "ants." These books were left in the book area or theme table for children to look at.

Susan does a letter "A" review with the ants books and the children play a game with the flannel board where they pick up a body part and put it in place on the flannel board. Figure 3.4 shows the flannel board ant parts.

Tues.	Weds.	Thurs.	Fri.
WHAT ARE ANTS?	ANTS ARE INSECTS	BIG & SMALL ANTS	COUNT ANTS
Informational book on ants in circle time	Ants are bugs & compare bugs with animals using pictures	Book - "Who can't follow an ant"	Review song and books Read *Ant Cities*
Flannel board ant body part game	Read other ant books	Do size words ants are "big" ants are "small"	Counting ant games
		Sorting ants by size	Guess how many ants
What do ants eat project outside	Go outside to check ant food choices	Make antennas and have an ant parade	Finger paint ants
Ant items in centers	Cooking activity Ants on a log		

Children can match words to parts. "Sam, this word is leg. Can you find the ant's leg?"

Susan and Dan take the children outside to place dishes with various foods to see what ants like to eat (sugar, honey, bologna, celery etc.).

They sing the ant marching song and collect their observations for the next day's circle time and further activities in the centers.

Day 3. Ants Are Bugs

Susan starts the circle time by rereading *Two bad ants*. Susan explains what an insect is and engages children in a game where they pick up the bug or animal pictures. She uses pictures of insects and animals cut out of magazines for this game.

They go outside to check the food trays and talk about what the ants liked to eat. When they come back inside and go to the centers, there are plastic ants in the sandbox for children to play with.

Later, they cook "ants on a log" using celery sticks with peanut butter on top and raisins stuck on the peanut butter (raisins are the ants). In the music center, they listen to a tape Susan made of the song, "March of the worker ants" (Oram, Davis, & Kitamura, 1993).

Day 4. Ants Big and Small

She reads the story *Who can't follow an ant?* (Pellowski, 1986). They reread *Two bad ants* and talk

about what they know about ants now versus when they first listened to the story.

Susan and Dan introduce a game based on size. Are ants "big" or "small?" Children are asked to "pick up the large ant" (or "small ant") and put it in a basket. These are ants made out of construction paper, Styrofoam, felt, or whatever materials you can locate. Dan passes different sized ants around to the children and says, "If you have a little ant, (or big ant) stand up." Following this activity, Susan plays music and the children, pretending they are ants, crawl around based on Dan's instructions: "Ants are running (sniffing, eating etc.)."

They go outside to check the food trays and talk about what the ants liked to eat.

In the art center, the children make ant antennas using pipe cleaners. Susan plays the "Ants go marching" song and the children sing and march to the song. The words to the song are displayed in large letters in the circle time area to help develop connections between print and speech.

In the closing circle time activity, Susan introduces the alphabet book, *Antics* (Hepworth, 1992).

Day 5. Counting Ants

Susan introduces the days activities by reading from a book introduced on day 2. She reads the section of *Ant cities* (Dorros, 1987) that suggests ants build cities of various sizes.

There are small ant cities with just a few ants.
There are big ant cities with many, many ants.
Ants have been found at the tops of the highest buildings and on ships at sea. (Dorros, p. 30)

Using the ants made for the big and small ant activity on day 4, Susan and Dan play counting games. "Can you pick up one ant?" "Can you put three ants in the bucket?" "Can you count two ants with your finger (on the flannel board)?"

They ask the children to "guess how many ants are in the ant farm?"

Sam says, "seven-hundred." Naijala says, "a hundred." Bob says, "three" Jack says, "ten."

Dan records the children's guesses on a large paper with their names.

In art, they fingerpaint ants by dipping the tip of their finger in paint to make dot bodies of ants. They add legs, antennas, and other body parts with markers. Figure 3.5 displays children's ant body finger painting.

Children can make up actions for their finger paint ants and dictate these captions for you to write. "My ants are eating bread." "The ants are going home." "The ants like sugar."

Throughout this week long unit on ants, each of the centers features ant-related materials. Children can bring in materials for the ant unit too. It is fairly easy

Figure 3.4. Ant Part Activity

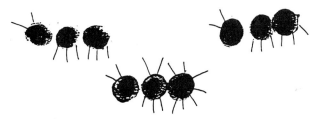

Figure 3.5. Ant Finger Painting Activity

to find books and songs about ants, but you can also let your imagination run wild and create many of your own materials for this unit. The children's constructions such as the finger painting activity can become part of a book they make to take home to their families. Do not confine yourself to a week if children's interest is still there. Or, you can build on this unit to include other insects. When you have concluded your unit, put it all away in a box for future use. Ants never go out of style!

Children's learning about the joys and functions of reading and writing grows naturally through thematic units that link their interests with print. Songs, dramatic play, listening to stories, drawing, labeling, games, and enjoying the outdoor environment all combine to make their journey toward language an exciting voyage of discovery.

In this last section, we suggest additional resource books and read aloud selections we like to use. This list is brief and selective, rather than long. Most contemporary books on children's literature, however, include easy-to-browse CD-ROMs and diskette databases of books by theme, age-appropriate level, and other categories.

Libraries have age appropriate lists and librarians are great sources for old favorites and new books.

We also include some software suggestions from the growing library of computer-assisted books, simulations, and materials. Finally, we mention some of the many excellent books that can help you design a print enriched preschool environment.

RESOURCES

Teacher resource books:

Allen, D. D., & Piersma, M. L. (1995). *Developing thematic units: Process and product.* New York: Delmar.

Beaty, J. J. (1992). *Preschool appropriate practices.* Fort Worth, TX: Harcourt, Brace, Jovanovich.

Dodge, D. T., & Colker, L. J. (1995). *The creative curriculum for early childhood* (3rd. Ed.). Washington, DC: Teaching Strategies Inc.

Jacobs, J. S., & Tunnell, M. O. (1996). *Children's literature briefly.* Englewood Cliffs, NJ: Merrill.

Johnson, P. (1990). *A book of one's own: Developing literacy through making books.* Portsmouth, NH: Heinemann.

Lawler-Prince, D., Altieri, J. L., & Cramer, M. M. (1996). *Moving toward an integrated curriculum in early childhood education.* Washington D. C.: National Education Association.

Morrow, L. M. (1993). *Literacy development in the early years* (2nd Ed.). Boston, MA: Allyn and Bacon.

Spodek, B. (1993). *Handbook of research on the education of young children.* New York: Macmillan.

Terzian, A. M. (1993). *The kids' multicultural art book.* Charlotte, VE: Williamson Publishing.

Predictable and Interactive Books:

Agell, C. (1994). *Dancing feet.* San Diego, CA: Harcourt.

Anno, M. (1977). *Anno's counting book.* New York: HarperCollins.

Aruego, J., & Dewey, A. (1979). *We hide, you seek.* New York: Greenwillow.

Arnosky, J. (1994). *All night near the water.* New York: Putnam.

Balian, L. (1972). *The animal.* Nashville, Tennessee: Abingdon.

Barrett, J., & Barrett, R. (1970). *Animals should definitely not wear clothing.* New York: Macmillan.

Bayer, J., & Kellogg, S. (1984). *A my name is ALICE.* New York: Dial.

Bender, R. (1994). *A most unusual lunch.* New York: Dial.

Bennett, J., & dePaola, T. (1986). *Teeny tiny.* New York: Putnam.

Blos, J. W. (1992). *A seed a flower a minute, an hour.* New York: Simon & Schuster.

Bornstein, R. (1976). *Little Gorilla.* New York: Clarion.

Brouillard, A. (1992). *Three cats.* Charlottesville, Virginia: Thomasson-Grant.

Brown, M. W. (1947). *Goodnight moon.* New York: Harper.

Brown, R. (1981). *A dark dark tale.* New York: Dial.

Burningham, J. (1970). *Mr. Gumpy's outing.* New York: Holt.

Carle, E. (1992). *Draw me a star.* New York: Philomel.

Carle, E. (1968). *1, 2, 3, to the zoo: A counting book.* New York: Philomel.

Carle, E. (1969). *A very hungry caterpillar.* New York: Philomel.

Carle, E. (1990). *The very quiet cricket.* New York: Philomel.

Carle, E. (1996). *Little cloud.* New York: Philomel.

Carlstrom, N. W., & Sorensen, H. (1993). *What does the rain play?* New York: Macmillan.

Chapman, C. (1993). *Pass the fritters, critters.* New York: Four Winds.

Crews, D. (1978). *Freight train.* New York: Greenwillow.

Crews, D. (1995). *Sail away.* New York: Greenwillow.

Crews, N. (1995). *One hot summer day.* New York: Greenwillow.

Crimi, C. (1995). *Outside, inside.* New York: Simon & Schuster.

Dussling, J. (1996). *Stars.* New York: Grossert & Dunlap.

Fleming, D. (1993). *In the small small pond.* New York: Holt.

Freeman, D. (1986). *Corduroy.* New York: Puffin.

Gray, L. M. (1995). *My mama had a dancing heart.* New York: Orchard.

Hamanaka, S. (1994). *All the colors of the earth*. New York: Morrow.

Helldorfer, H. (1994). *Gather up, gather in: A book of seasons*. New York: Viking.

Hopkins, L. B. (1995). *Good rhymes, good times*. New York: HarperCollins.

Iverson, D. (1993). *I celebrate nature*. Nevada City, CA: Dawn.

Jeunesse, G., & de Bourgoing, P. (1992) *Discovery books* (The tree, weather etc.). New York: Scholastic.

Jonas, A. (1989). *Color dance*. New York: Greenwillow.

Kalan, R. (1981). *Jump, frog, jump!* New York: Scholastic.

Kasza, K. (1992). *A mother for Choco*. New York: Putnam.

Kitamura, S. (1986). *When sheep cannot sleep: The counting book*. New York: Farrar Straus Giroux.

Krauss, R. (1945). *The carrot seed*. New York: Scholastic.

Lionni, L. (1959). *Little blue and little yellow*. New York: Scholastic.

Lionni, L. (1973). *Swimmy*. New York: Random House.

Luenn, N. (1992). *Mother earth*. New York: Aladdin.

Martin, B., & Archambault, J. (1988). *Listen to the rain*. New York: Holt.

Martin, B., & Carle, E. (1964). *Brown bear, brown bear, what do you see?* New York: Holt.

Maas, R. (1993). *When winter comes*. New York: Holt.

McMullan, K. (1996). *If you were my bunny*. New York: Scholastic.

Numeroff, L. J. (1985). *If you give a mouse a cookie*. New York: Harper.

Ockenga, S., & Doolittle, E. (1987). *The ark in the attic: An alphabet adventure*. Boston, MA: Godine.

Pinkey, J. (1994). *Max found two sticks*. New York: Simon & Schuster.

Regan, D. C. (1996). *Mommies*. New York: Scholastic.

Rockwell, A. (1994). *Ducklings and pollywogs*. New York: Macmillan.

Rosen, M. (1989). *We're going on a bear hunt*. New York: McElderry.

Sardegna, J. (1994). *K is for kiss good night: A bedtime alphabet*. New York: Doubleday.

Sendak, M. (1962). *Chicken soup with rice*. New York: Harper.

Shaw, N. (1986). *Sheep in a jeep*. New York: Houghton Mifflin.

Soto, G. (1991). *Mama do you love me?* New York: Putnam.

Soto, G. (1993). *Too many tamales*. New York: Putnam.

Zolotow, C. (1995). *When the wind stops*. New York: HarperCollins.

Other Resources:

The National Association for the Education of Young Children offers additional materials in all areas of early childhood curriculum including the journal, *Young Children*. Write to:

NAEYC
1509 16th Street, N. W.
Washington, DC 20036-1426
Phone: 1-800-424-2460 or (202) 232-8777
Fax: (202) 328-1946

Books from the Ant Unit

Beall, P. (1996). The ants go marching. *Wee sing silly songs*. New York: Putnam.

Dorros, A. (1987). *Ant cities*. New York: Thomas Y. Crowell.

Hepworth, C. (1992). *Antics*. New York: Putnam.

Oram, H., Davis, C., & Kitamura, S. (1993). *A creepy crawly song book*. New York: Farrar, Straus, and Giroux.

Overbeck, C. (1982). *Ants*. Minneapolis, MN: Lerner.

Pellowski, M. J. (1986). *Who can't follow an ant*. New York: Troll.

Van Allsburg, C. (1988). *Two bad ants*. Boston, MA: Houghton Mifflin.

An Internet Web Page for Bugs

Gordon's Entomological Home Page address:

http://www.ex.ac.uk/~gjlramel/welcome.html

This resource features an online collection of bugs ranging from spiders and insects to arthropods and mites. You can ask an expert questions you have about bugs, join a bug club, and link to other bug resources.

REFERENCES

Allen, D. D., & Piersma, M. L. (1995). *Developing thematic units: Process and product*. New York: Delmar.

Britsch, S. (1993). Experience & literacy. *Instructor*. Nov./Dec., 48-49.

Carle, E. (1996). *Little cloud*. New York: Philomel.

Crews, N. (1995). *One hot summer day*. New York: Greenwillow.

Essa, E. (1996). *Introduction to early childhood education* (2nd Ed.). Albany, NY: Delmar.

Gillet, J. W., & Temple, C. (1994). *Understanding reading problems: Assessment and instruction* (4th Ed.). New York: Harper/Collins.

Kalan, R. (1981). *Jump, frog, jump*. New York: Scholastic.

Martin, B., & Carle, E. (1983). *Brown bear, brown bear, what do you see?* New York: Holt.

Numeroff, L. J. (1985). *If you give a mouse a cookie*. New York: Harper.

Rybczynski, M., & Troy, A. (1995). Literacy enriched play centers: Trying them out in "the real world." *Childhood Education*, Fall, 7-12.

Vygotsky, L. S. (1962). *Thought and language*. New York: John Wiley & Sons.

Walker, B. J. (1996). *Diagnostic teaching of reading: Techniques for instruction and assessment* (3rd Ed.). Englewood Cliffs, NJ: Prentice Hall.

CHAPTER 4

Emerging Readers and Writers in Kindergarten

Children who come into kindergarten have had many experiences with reading and writing. Many of them attended preschools and day care centers, hopefully rich in experiences with print. We like to think of kindergarten as the year children emerge and grow as readers and writers, even though their experiences with print may vary quite a bit. In kindergarten, we want them to bloom as readers and writers, just like flowers, each slightly different, opening or emerging at different times and in different ways. Teachers, parents, and other caregivers provide the support for children to grow into literacy. We water, feed, weed, and hope they bloom, just as we do with flowers. Oh, and we also have *patience*, the key ingredient whether you are growing readers, writers, or flowers!

In this chapter we present our ideas on how to organize a kindergarten program that encourages readers and writers. We will discuss these ideas:

▌ Life before kindergarten
▌ A plan for organizing the time, space, and resources available to you in both half-day and full-day kindergartens
▌ How to tie one day to the next and weave activities together using theme teaching
▌ How to keep track of what you do day-by-day and assess how children's reading and writing emerges.

LIFE BEFORE KINDERGARTEN

The children below all may come into the same kindergarten, each child with years of experiences with language from different environments. Some are natural readers and writers, while others will need more support and encouragement. Let's have a look at where these children come from...[1]

Latisha goes to her grandmother's house each morning where she watches some television, draws and paints, and often helps her Nana cook lunch. Then it is off to Buttons and Bows Day Care for the afternoon until one of her parents picks her up after work. Latisha's favorite presents come from numerous aunts and uncles who give her toys and many books. She has an older computer to use at home for games and simple word processing. Latisha's dolls and books are carefully arranged in her room and she talks regularly to her dolls and reads them stories, often assuming different voices for each character in a story. She sorts her books into piles on the floor, naming each one as she places them in some category known only to her. After carefully sorting them in stacks, she then asks her dolls which book they would like to hear.

"Oh, I don't think you want me to read that one," she will say, if she is in the mood for a longer book

session. "I know one you want to hear. It's my best book! It says, 'Are you my mother?" It has a big 'Snort' in it. See that?" and she holds the book open so the dolls can see the illustrations. Then she picks one doll, again, according to her own private criteria, places it in her lap, and talks to the doll and acts out a story with it. Her dolls become the different characters and assume the character's voices in the story she's acting out.

Beatriz goes to a neighborhood daycare house for the whole day with four or five other preschoolers. They play games, watch television for part of the day, work on arts and crafts projects related to holidays, birthdays, or special events. The children are read a story or two, usually before rest periods. At the end of the day, Beatriz's older brother picks her up and takes her home. She is the youngest of three children and her two older brothers are "in charge" when their parents are at work. Spanish and English are spoken in the home, with much shifting back and forth between languages. One brother posts messages on the refrigerator door about a special parent event at the day care center to raise money for the toy box fund, next week's lunch menu, and a reminder that volunteers are needed to help with crafts projects. He reads these to Beatriz and they talk about the lunch choices for next week, especially the foods she doesn't really like. Beatriz posts a drawing she did today for all to see on the refrigerator door, goes to her room, plays by herself with her dolls and listens to some song tapes she likes over and over. When her mother comes home, they eat and discuss Beatriz's day, a story gets read to her by someone and off to bed—another day in the life of a four-year-old.

David sits on his potty reading a book. At three years his chubby legs, bent to accommodate the low seat, form a comfortable lap for his book. He looks at the pictures by touching different parts of them and then carries on a "conversation" with the characters in the story. Then he "reads" the page. His story follows the pictures closely each time he reads it. Before he turns the page, David sometimes plays a little guessing game and talks to a character by saying, "I'll bet you don't know what's gonna happen next..., but I do!" Then he turns the page and continues the story. David spent his preschool years at home and has one younger brother and an older sister who is in kindergarten. David's mother has wished a thousand times that he would take care of "first things first." After all, whoever heard of reading in wet training pants? David seems to be perfectly satisfied with the way things are. He is a natural reader.

Jon[2] has a moderate hearing loss and during the mornings he attends a preschool program for the hearing impaired in a public school. His speech can be understood and he talks in phrases and sentences.

Different children have varying experiences with reading before kindergarten.

Each day, the teacher completes a simple experience chart story with the children. There are lots of books available in the room, along with other kinds of print for children to browse through. Other daily routines include calendar activities, show-and-tell, and specific lessons in oral and sign language, e.g. naming parts of the body. Jon is struggling to learn to read and spell his name through a variety of activities. He chooses his name card from among several others but it is hard to tell if this is a good guess or if Jon really recognizes his name. The teacher writes his name on a drawing he completed and Jon very carefully and slowly copies it under her model. When the teacher looks in on Jon a few moments later, he has painted over the name she wrote and written his own a second time. Jon is sending a strong message, "This is my work, I am the owner of it, and my name represents me and my work!"

Anna is from Bosnia and she and her twin brother came to the United States with many early encounters and experiences in their native language which is not English. Anna is so curious; her eyes are everywhere and she listens to her teacher very carefully. Once an activity begins, Anna's eyes turn left and right to see what other children are doing and then she begins, modeling what she does after what others are doing. Her work is like a quilt patched together—a little from David, an idea from Homero, a dash of John, a touch of Susan, and a splash of Beatriz. When others read a picture book and make up stories from the pictures, Anna does too, moving her lips and softly reading outloud in her native language as her eyes run across the English print, then dart to the child

reading on her left or right. As each child finishes, so does Anna, never first, but never last. She has very cleverly figured out what reading is all about by copying what the other children do. When the teacher reads a funny story in English, she laughs with the other children, too. Anna is on her way to acting like a reader, using the early experiences in her native country to guide her actions in her new country while she learns to read in a second language. Whew! She must have lots of energy, it sounds like a complex job to us.

Derek does not always join in activities early in the morning with the class. He may be physically present in the room each day, but he often appears mentally tired. For Derek, and for increasingly larger numbers of children, learning to read and write is not the major challenge of school life. He walks to school at 7:30 A.M. and sits on the curb outside the cafeteria area, waiting for the doors to open and for breakfast to be served. Even when it is cold, he is there, often sleepy, with hair uncombed, and clothes too light for the weather. His smile, freckles, blue eyes, and tousled blond hair would melt anyone's heart. He is full of the "blarney" as his older sister tells the teacher; gifted at pretending to be much older and wiser in life than his age. Neglected? Hmm, depends. Derek's dad comes to every school play, scheduled meetings for parents, and makes impromptu visits. Derek brings toys and family items for sharing time. Home for Derek sometimes may be the back seat of a car for the evening while an adult works nearby, or a couch at a relative's house when it is offered. Early experiences with print at home? Not regularly, but he has plenty of experiences with life. Derek's eagerness and willingness to learn will support him as he learns to read and write. Many of the experiences he has not had with reading and writing will fall to the kindergarten teacher to provide for him—those hundreds of hours of easy and informal experiences some children have at home or in preschools.

Kindergarten programs must be considered as big umbrellas where children with a wide range of individual differences can fit—otherwise some children will be excluded right from the beginning. Like flowers, some are buds, while others are already opening with a hint of color and size to come. For more and more children in our country, their life experiences overshadow their experiences with print. Kindergarten programs must accept, respect, and use the life, home, day care, and preschool experiences children like Latisha, Beatriz, David, Jon, Anna and Derek have had. It is our job to use that foundation of experiences as a bridge to their emerging as readers and writers.

Easy to say, but, how can you really build a kindergarten program for 20 or 25 or more children based on their experiences when they all seem so different? Actually their experiences with reading and writing may be different, but what they *learn* from these early encounters with print is not all that different. They slowly become aware that print:

▌ Means or tells something.
▌ Has lots of uses, because it shows us how to find things we like, such as favorite foods, lets us give messages to other people, tells us important stuff.
▌ Goes a certain way, left to right, top to bottom, has pages and lines.
▌ Helps us gain control over our world because it is dependable—a sign or label goes the same way and says the same thing time after time.
▌ Goes together with talk—adults spend a lot of time talking about things they read by themselves and with us.
▌ Means fun and laughter, too, especially the stories we hear and we read together.

Next, we will present some ways of organizing, planning, and assessing activities in your kindergarten classroom. Before we begin, we cannot promise to tell you everything you have ever wanted to know about teaching kindergarten. What we will try to do is to get you off to a good start, and you and the children take it from there.

The rest of this chapter is organized around these four steps in planning your kindergarten program:

1. Follow a plan and organize time, space and resources available to you.
2. Tie one day to the next, weaving one activity with another.

3. Keep track of what you do.
4. Evaluate what you do over time.

A PLAN FOR ORGANIZING TIME, SPACE, AND RESOURCES AVAILABLE TO YOU

How are we going to help these children grow as "readers and writers?" It is easy to get bogged down in details and worry about "what am I going to do." Before you start *doing* activities, one after another, remember the old saying, "Can't see the forest for the trees." Without some idea of *where* you are going to guide your decisions of *what* to do each day, your kindergarten will become activity-oriented, with you spending too much time planning, building, cutting and pasting, gluing, and doing most of the work. Remember, also, *you* can read and write, your students are just learning—they should work harder than you work! Right?

In the next section of this chapter, we present some basic plans for you to consider. We selected these plans from the many available for teachers to use. We tried to pick those daily plans that met the guidelines for what is known as *developmentally appropriate literacy instruction*[3] developed by the National Association for the Education of Young Children, updated to include some newer ideas. Developmentally appropriate instruction reflects the best practices we know for helping young children grow as readers and writers. Recently, some educators have urged us to expand our ideas about what is developmentally appropriate and allow teachers to use all kinds of teaching strategies, as long as they result in children reading and writing for authentic purposes. These practices should include activities and experiences that meet these standards:

The teacher should encourage reading and writing every day.

1. The whole child should be involved in literacy instruction. Children need activities that use their bodies and their minds, engages them in active not passive tasks and includes many opportunities for working and playing together. These physical, emotional, social, and cognitive parts of the whole child should all be challenged throughout the school day.
2. Talking, reading, and writing activities should be integrated, that is, woven together like a cloth, with activities related to each other as much as possible.
3. Activities should be relevant or mean something to young children. Their levels of thinking and physical abilities must be considered when planning activities.
4. Activities should be woven together and involve choice and self-selection by children, in addition to those activities chosen by teachers.
5. The teacher, the expert reader and writer in the room, should model and demonstrate reading and writing each day.
6. The teacher works first *with* children to support and guide them before they try their wings as emerging readers and writers (for those psychologists among you, Vygotsky[4] would be pleased with these kinds of activities).
7. Children should practice reading, writing, and talking in many ways—alone, in pairs and small groups, and as a whole class, while you watch and see how they do on their own.
8. Skills and strategies for becoming independent readers and writers can be taught in meaningful ways that engage children's interests.

Here are some simple plans for a kindergarten curriculum. You may pick and choose from these plans to get started and later change them slowly to make them work for you. Keep in mind that some kindergartens are on half-day and others are full-day schedules. We will present a bare bones outline of a basic plan for both as a place to start. A basic plan that includes daily routines is very important for both the children and for you, too. Children depend on you to create a stable learning environment; you need one for your mental health. There are enough surprises you cannot plan for each day in teaching, so at least start each day with a good, solid, dependable plan— add the fancy sauces and desserts later!

THE BARE-BONES PLAN FOR HALF-DAY KINDERGARTEN

Getting Started with Opening Routines. Each day should begin with some settling-in and opening routines. As children come into the room, greet them and have them find or write their names. Early in the year they can find their pictures among those pasted on cards on a pegboard. Each child finds the correct picture and turns it over to find his or her name. The pictures can be brought from home by each child or taken by the teacher in school. Later in the year, the children can sign in by their names on a large piece of chart paper with spaces for a whole week.

Next, the children can gather around the teacher on the floor in a rough semi-circle. The teacher sits near the monthly calendar and a chart holder with a blank sheet of chart paper on it. Children volunteer to find the day of the week and its number and name. Other children can volunteer the names the days before and after today, along with their numbers. A few moments of share-and-tell come next, with birthdays being mentioned and noted with a birthday song, teeth that have been lost can be recorded on the lost tooth tally chart on the wall, something special that happened in a child's life (I got a new pair of shoes) is mentioned, or a holiday or special school event coming up is volunteered. The teacher can share an event or something of interest, too. If a science project is underway that involves growing seeds or some other activity where changes can be observed, these can be noted by the children and recorded, too. The teacher can choose any of these events and record them on chart paper, modeling writing for the children. As they learn more about words and letters, individual children can volunteer to re-read the chart, locate certain names or words, or find specific letters in words.

Reading and Writing with the Children. While the children are still gathered around the teacher, it is now time for the teacher to read a story or poem, tell a story, or share something else related to an on-going activity or theme study, from a newspaper, magazine, or reference book. If animals are being studied, then pick an informational or funny story about an animal to read and discuss. At first, try to select stories that can be read in one sitting. As the year goes on, however, pick some stories that are carried forward to the next day. Do not forget Nancy Larrick's reminder—"Keep a poem in your pocket." Sometimes a poem is just right for a holiday, special event, seasonal changes, or just for fun (Larrick, 1987). It is important to keep a record of stories read to the children on a large chart for the whole year. As the list grows, it can be reviewed every few weeks to see if children remember stories and make connections between them, such as those written by the same author or stories with the same theme. This year's list can be stored and brought out at the beginning of next year to show children how many stories they will hear during the year.

Try telling a story occasionally to the students. Read it ahead of time, rehearse it once or twice, and then tell it to the children.

Reading and re-reading books with children, or the repeated readings of their favorite books helps their progress toward becoming a 'real reader.' Sulzby and her colleagues (1993) have shown that children's efforts to read can be encouraged if they are given many invitations to "read it the kindergarten way," "read it your own way," and "sure you can do it," followed by praise for trying to read. Same for writing, by encouraging them to write a story in their own way and praising their efforts to write real messages, children gain the confidence to keep writing.

A story record or tape can also be used during this time. If there is a tape and a book that go together, use them both, then they can be placed in the reading center for children to listen to again on their own. Many good commercial tapes of stories can be purchased. We like more personal ones with readers' voices the children easily recognize. Ask the principal, nurse, physical education teacher, music teacher, crossing guard, bus drivers, cafeteria helpers and other staff to tape stories for your classroom library. Grandmothers and grandfathers also can be pressed into service, with those far away sending a tape by mail for the class. In one school partnership we found, senior citizens in an adult day care facility became regular readers on tape of good stories for children. Local officials and media personalities can also be invited to add a reader tape to the classroom or school library.

Tie reading to writing and have the children end this part of the day by writing with you. For example, if they have just heard a story taped by someone, they can draw an illustration for the story, write a thank-you note to the person who read the story, or dictate a whole-group-experience-thank-you-note while you write it and they sign all their names. Their thank-you-notes can be mailed or delivered to the person who read the tape. Whatever writing is done should have a real purpose, and not be just for the teacher. A simple classroom newsletter can be prepared and distributed to other kindergarten classes in the building and sent home to parents. Children can work together to get various parts of the newsletter ready such as interviewing the principal about important school events to come, reporting on classroom activities, asking for parent or adult volunteers to help with a project, and other topics can be included in the newsletter. As the children's writing becomes more fluent, they can take over more and more of the newsletter responsibilities. The computer or typewriter is a great help here for little hands that cannot quite get those letters right just yet.

The more practice children get, the more their writing skills develop.

Children might listen to a story or view a videotape and then record what they have learned, either by themselves or dictated to you. While growing seeds, their observations about how to care for the seeds and how the seeds grow can form a science log chart. Writing down recipes used in the housekeeping center and illustrating a kindergarten book of favorite recipes over time is another writing project that can be shared with other classes and parents.

Wondering about how much writing children can do at this age that is legible and can actually be read by someone else? Worry not, their emerging writing develops quickly the more practice children get. They will go from scribbling and what looks like random scrawls to you (but really are messages if you ask them to read them back to you) to personal or invented spellings as they try to spell words by the way they sound. With experience, children move rapidly to more conventional or familiar spelling throughout the year. We will discuss this shift from personal spelling to familiar or conventional spelling in the next chapter. The more writing you do with them and the more writing they do on their own, the faster the movement to regular spelling will be. By February, in one classroom we observed, when a student finished writing something, the teacher would ask, "Do you want to read it to me or shall I read it to you?" as a student's writing became easier to figure out. As students felt confident enough, they would say, "You read it to me," and the teacher usually asked other students to join her and celebrate the reading. At the end of the day, during the closing routine, the teacher might also comment on how much he or she enjoyed reading a student's work during the day.

Movement and Motion, Music, Play and a Snack. Time flies, but little bodies need to stretch and move. This is a good time for some body-awareness activities that can be combined with a song (sung by you or on tape) that involves touching your toes, your nose, elbows, closing your eyes and your ears, standing on one foot, raising your right hand and then your left hand—get the idea? A snack and restroom break also are in order right about now.

Learning by Doing: Center Time. The pre-school chapter you read earlier had many good suggestions for centers. We add a few more here for kindergarten classrooms. Teachers new to using centers may want to start opening centers one at a time, gradually adding and introducing new centers. Jewell and Zintz (1990) reminds us that young children should be given preparation for the use of centers. They should know the reason for them, and they should be shown how to care for, clean up, and return materials to their proper places. Jewell and Zintz suggest a "practice walk through" with children before they begin to work in centers. A small group can be introduced to the writing center, for example, and be shown all the writing supplies and where to put things back in their proper places. An older child or volunteer can also help the teacher supervise centers as children learn to use them.

As with all learning, we would add: repeat directions and demonstrate how to use a center several times if children appear confused or do not replace materials. To help manage the traffic flow in your classroom, you might want to keep all centers open some days, and only specific ones on other days. Announce what centers are open at the beginning of center time. Children can choose centers and will generally move around to different ones. Some teachers pre-assign centers for each child, but we find that cumbersome. If a child appears to stick to one center too long, suggest that he or she try another center and move along. We like to suggest that as the year goes on and more writing and reading emerge, the teacher can pull a small group of children aside for five or ten minutes and do some guided reading and writing or skills and strategies lessons in small groups or individually. It is also a good time to use some of the in-formal assessments we will discuss later in this chapter.

A small group of children who might be having trouble with naming the letters of the alphabet might be pulled together and away from their center activities for five to ten minutes for a review of letter names. A child who is struggling with forming certain letters while writing might get a few minutes of individual instruction and practice with the teacher or with an aide. Once the children begin to read simple pattern and predictable books (see *Resources* section of this for more information on pattern and predictable books), the teacher can pull together small groups with similar abilities, and conduct a guided reading in less than ten minutes with the following steps:[5]

1. Introduce the new little book by previewing the title and having children page through it looking at the pictures and discussing them briefly.
2. Read the little book to the children asking them to follow along and read orally with you, if they can.
3. Have the students read the story a second time, this time while you read it orally and they read silently (or "Follow with your eyes as I read, please").
4. Ask the children to retell the simple story with you, using the pictures.
5. Students are then paired for a third reading on their own while you pull together another group to work with.
6. The next day, pull the group that read a new story the previous day and have them read it orally while you "shadow read," or read just a second or so behind them for support. Fade out as the children read more fluently. Remind them to point to the words and slide their fingers along the line of print until they get the idea.
7. Additional readings can occur until the children seem fluent. Read the story to them orally while they follow along silently; try another paired reading. Finally, pair yourself with a child who seems to be struggling and give some one-to-one attention.
8. As children become more comfortable with their reading of little books in small groups, introduce some strategies by demonstrating how the children can figure out a word they do not know by themselves: a) use the picture clues to help you with a new word; b) point and slide along the line of print to keep your place; c) try going back and re-reading when you get stuck; d) point to the first letter in a word you do not know, get your mouth ready and try the first sound; e) go on to the next word, it might help you. One way to remind students of these strategies is to post

a simple list of steps to follow near the area where you meet with small groups:

<u>What Do You Do When You Get Stuck?</u>
Go back. Try again.
Use the pictures.
Point to the word.
Get your mouth ready and try to sound it out.
Does it make sense?
Were you right?

9. Encourage children to try new strategies, "What should you do when you come to a word you don't know?" "Show me how you figured out the word," or "How did you know you were right?"
10. Praise the children as soon as you notice they have tried a strategy, "Good checking, you used the pictures to help you." "I saw you pointing and sounding the word."

Let the children use a computer to help them with their writing.

When you are not working with the children in small groups or individually, circulate around the room. Real 'teaching points' will jump out at you. One child will need help spelling a word, getting a drawing started, forming a letter, or remembering part of the story read this morning. Sometimes they need just a pat on the back for a job well done. In one story we watched a teacher read with a small group of children, the words "sunrise" and "bedtime" were part of a simple story. The teacher wrote the words on a chart and asked, "What are the two little words in sunrise?" A short lesson on compound words followed.

Here are some suggestions for centers we know work. Use others as you find and develop ideas for them. Most centers do not need to change all that frequently. Other centers need sprucing up once in a while.

Reading and Writing Center: You can divide this center into halves, splitting the space you have between reading and writing. Some classrooms have separate centers for reading and writing. We think the message to kids should be that reading and writing go together, so we put them in one big center.

For the reading side, you and the children should collect books of all kinds. The *Resources* section of this chapter contains lists of specific titles and sources of print to include in this center. If an author study is underway for a week or so, then all the books you can find by the author can be included in one place in the reading and writing center. A section of books related to a theme under study can be included and changed as the theme does. Especially important are ABC or alphabet books, number or counting books, and the

books you and the children publish in the classroom. Include other kinds of print, too, such as magazines for kids, restaurant menus, phone books, picture dictionaries, and other kinds of everyday print. Also, talk with the school librarian, or visit the local public library or book store children's book sections and ask about good books to include. Usually the sales people in a children's book store are very eager to help.

For the writing side, stock the center with lots of paper of all kinds and writing tools such as pencils, crayons and markers. Keep your computer here, if you have one, so children can learn to use it for their writing. If you have no computer, find a typewriter. Both can be used when the children publish a book of their own. Try to create the reading and writing center where you also have wall space to display children's writing.

Finally, children can dictate or write and illustrate their own stories and make them into simple books in the reading and writing center. A parent volunteer, or aide, can help with this activity and assemble the books using simple bindings of yarn and a hole-punch, or by folding and gluing. Some of these books can be sent to the school library and displayed in a separate section reserved for books published by students in the school.

Math Center: Math occurs in many places during the day. For example, the calendar used when doing the day of the week during the opening routine we discussed earlier is displayed during the day in the math center. Keep in the center, the room calendar and wall chart with a week-by-week record of lost teeth, along with any other charts on which you record information using numbers. This center can contain the tools you need to demonstrate math concepts and for children to practice these concepts. Include items such as: math manipulatives, supplies for cutting, pasting, and making shapes and objects, counting and pattern blocks of all kinds, construction paper, rulers, play money, and a few real coins.

Play Center: Play centers are just as important in kindergarten as they are in preschool. Refer to the preschool chapter for ideas for a play center. We suggest this center be an impromptu stage, ready at a moment's notice to be turned into a puppet theater, or place for a skit based on a story just read or told. Keep simple rhythm instruments here, a box of clothes for "dress up" costumes, cassette player or record player and a small collection of all kinds of music — marches, classical, holiday, and current songs (with earphones, too, for private listening), a play telephone, and any other props you collect over the years. Some teachers also include a housekeeping corner in this play center with child-sized kitchen equipment. What you include in your classroom depends on how much space and budget you have. Creating a mini-home environment that combines a play kitchen and utensils with table and chairs for dining is a great place to generate interactive play. Keep recipe books here and a note pad and paper by the play phone for those special messages. Encourage the students to write and post messages for each other on the refrigerator door or bulletin board in this area using post-it notes or with magnets.

Art Center: Cover the floor, cover the floor, cover the floor under this center before you do another thing! Place a small, two-sided easel with chart paper on each side and some crayons and watercolor paints in this center along with a variety of colored construction paper and children's scissors. These basic ingredients will give the children a place to illustrate stories and to experiment with drawing and coloring, and just for "making stuff." You can add other art supplies for special projects related to a theme or unit of study as needed.

Discovery Center: This center supports themes, or units of study, underway in the classroom with special emphasis on social studies and science activities. It will change more frequently than others as you move from theme to theme in science and social studies. For example, while a desert unit is underway, the center will contain items mostly related to the desert; real things such as seed pods, a cactus plant, and other objects from the desert. A videotape on a topic under study might also be found here. After a visit by a special resource person, such as someone talking about bicycle safety, the center can be organized by the children around that topic as a follow-up to the visit.

Any More Room? At this point you may wonder how we can put anything else in the room. Of course it would be nice to have a large blocks area, toy area, a sand and water table, and on and on. Some of these can be placed outside the classroom (especially the sand and water stuff!); but an area with large blocks is useful for encouraging play. Use your judgment about whether you have room for this equipment; if so, go ahead and create an area.

Closing Routines: Clean Up and Let's Go Home Time! Remember, the children made the mess so let them clean it up. Try not to be an obsessive neatnick — the children will learn to clean up as you show them how and expect them to do it. You can assign regular tasks, weekly or monthly, and have the children work in twos or threes. This saves time so you will not have to re-assign tasks in case one child is absent physically or mentally for a day.

We like the day to end by both the teacher and the children sharing about what happened today in kindergarten. The teacher can begin by modeling the type of sharing, for example, "Here's something I learned today — you all really enjoyed our story about Boris and Morris, and so did I. I really liked the part where…" or "I learned that some of you are one year older today!" or "What do you have to do to get ready for tomorrow?" "By the way, what day is tomorrow?" "Remember to take your notes home — three more days for picture money." "Here's what I am going to do with the rest of my day — today is my mother's birthday and we are having a party tonight at my house."

Stressing what you learned today and what you have to do to get ready for tomorrow are two good sharing routines to begin in kindergarten. Adding items to bridge days by sharing what you will do before tomorrow gets children talking, too. Later in the year you can formally ask two questions: "What's one thing you learned today?" "What's something you have to do to get ready for tomorrow?" These questions help children reflect on their day and anticipate tomorrow.

THE BARE-BONES PLAN FOR A FULL-DAY KINDERGARTEN

Follow half-day plan above until the *Closing Routines.* You will not have to clean up the classroom as if the day is over. Center projects and activities can be picked up in the afternoon. Also, "special" classes such as physical education, music, library, computers, and others will occur sometime during the week in schools where there are full day kindergartens. If there are none regularly planned in your school because there are no teachers assigned to these classes, you might want to set aside some regular times for one or more of these special classes and conduct it yourself. Getting parent volunteers, especially for music and art, is a bonus for you and the children. The day can seem long at times, so try to schedule volunteers mid-morning and mid-afternoon.

Morning Closing Routine: Signal the children it is time to get the room ready so we can go to lunch. Put lids on things, pick up a bit, stop working at a good spot in your project. Next, rest room stops, hand washing, and back to the semicircle on the floor. Any special announcements can now be given. You can ask the children to share something from the morning, read a short poem or story to them, and off we go to line up and go to lunch.

Whole Group Activity Time

School schedules vary, but many have an active playtime outside, or in a gym area, for children after lunch. Once that time is over, off to the restrooms, washing of hands, and back to the classroom.

Rest and Relax

Little bodies need rest and after such a busy day; therefore, your children need some quiet time. Each child should find a space where they can lie. Many children bring a special blanket to school or gym mats can be used. Dim the lights a bit, put on some quiet music and relax with the children. Sit in a rocker or comfortable chair, take off your shoes and rest or do some quiet activity for 20 minutes or so. When time is up, turn off the music, bring on the lights and let children slowly come awake again. Some children need more time than others to "get with it again" and should be left alone and not rushed (remember Derek at the beginning of this chapter?).

Theme Center and Other Class Activities

Full day kindergartens allow teachers and children to spend more time developing a theme and with center activities. This section of the afternoon will take the biggest chunk of time. You can add more math, science, and social studies activities to each theme. Culminating activities can be longer and more involved. Also, the teacher can continue to work with individual children or small groups for guided reading or math lessons. Specific skill or strategy instruc-

tion can also occur during center activities as the teacher pulls a few children (see *Learning by Doing: Center Time* section of this chapter). Sometimes the whole class can come together as the teacher does a lesson for all the children who need it. These lessons can be as simple as presenting a basic skill such as capitalizing the first letter of a sentence, or as complex as a bicycle safety lesson. Changes in centers can be introduced, too, to the whole group at one time.

Be sure to allow a restroom break about mid-afternoon.

Celebrations and Surprises

Everyone loves celebrations and surprises. The teacher can encourage children who have completed a reading or writing activity to "celebrate" and share it with the group—a birthday card written for a grandmother, an art project just completed. The teacher can use this time for celebrations of birthdays and other significant events in the lives of children. On another day, in place of celebrations, a special surprise can be planned such as a new story read or told, a poem, a story record or tape, or introducing something new into the centers. If a new theme is about to be introduced the next day, the teacher can share something interesting with the children about the new theme. Visitors, especially parent or adult volunteers, who have a special talent, can be a wonderful surprise at this time. Having visitors come regularly and work with the children is a nice break for you, too.

Closing Routines

The end of the day routines should follow those we wrote about earlier in this chapter for ending the half-day kindergarten.

TIE ONE DAY TO THE NEXT, WEAVING ONE ACTIVITY WITH ANOTHER

Theme Teaching

You and your students need a purpose for what you do that carries you one day and then ties it to the next day. Nothing is more tiring than just doing and doing each day. There is lots to do, as we said—plenty of activities to fill the day or half-day—but we know if activities are woven together and have a purpose, children learn more and you can teach more, and not feel so tired. Remember our mantra, **"I can read and write, the students can't; they need to work harder than I do."** Your planning for what to read to the children, how to organize the centers, and what activities to select will go much smoother if you have a purpose for what you do. Tying activities together is often called cross-curricular, interdisciplinary, integrated teaching (lots of experts, too many to list, would be *very* pleased by this!). We suggest that one practical, we've-seen-it-done-by-lots-of-teachers way is to tie reading, writing, talking, thinking, playing, building, math, science, social studies, music, and art together by using themes.

Themes come in many forms. In some schools, there is a core of themes teachers are asked to use such as Our Neighborhood, Animals, The World Around Us, Counting Up and Up, The ABC's of Reading, Author Study (e.g. the books of a favorite children's author), Fantasy Books, and so on. In our half-day and full-day kindergarten basic plans, we gave you a structure to work with, now weave a theme into it. A theme can last a week or longer. In all the themes you do, tie in reading and writing activities. If the school has some canned themes with units to accompany, use them the first time around and see how they work. If the themes are broad and there are no specific activities for you to follow, then you will have to plan how a theme will play out in your classroom. Always include themes the children suggest, in addition to any you or the school may have ready to go.

Make sure every theme…

1. Has a literacy connection through using children's literature and other kinds of print, writing, and talking.
2. Uses several centers for activities related to the theme.
3. Involves home and families.
4. Taps children's personal experiences from in and out of school.
5. Allows for children to participate in the planning of theme activities.
6. Leaves a trail to remember it through the children's drawing, writing, and photographs.

So many themes and so little space in this chapter, but next we present a simple theme and how you can organize activities around it in your classroom. There are four simple steps to planning and organizing theme teaching. As you become more experienced with theme teaching, you can expand the steps.

Step 1. Introduce the theme through a song, a poem, story, or picture books.
Step 2. Read and write about the theme with the children.
Step 3. Develop independent activities in centers related to the theme.
Step 4. Plan a finale, or culminating activity, with the children.

Introduce a theme to organize activities.

The theme we have chosen crosses the generations: *Grandmothers and Grandfathers*. Let's see how to take our Bare-Bones plans and include theme activities. We think you will need about a week to do this theme. Yes, it can go longer, but that decision will come as you work with the children and see how it goes.

Step 1 - Introduce the Theme. Introduce the theme just after your opening routines and during the time set aside for *Reading and Writing with the Children*. For our Grandmothers and Grandfathers theme you might read two stories, one each day, that present different views of grandmothers and compares and contrasts them with the children. We suggest a few books with different kinds of grandmothers:

My Grandmother Has Black Hair *by Mary Hoffman and Joanna Burroughes (1988). New York: Dial Books. The grandmother in this book wants to be called by her first name, she cannot knit or cook for beans, drives a noisy old car, and has a very rude parrot for a pet. This is a great story of a somewhat unusual grandmother.*

Loop the Loop *by Barbara Dugan, pictures by James Stevenson (1992). New York: Greenwillow Books. Eleanor, the little girl in this story, adopts an old woman in a wheelchair who turns out to be quite a character with a very special talent for snapping a yo-yo just like a champion! An unlikely pair these two, but the story is well told and heart warming.*

Grandma According to Me *by Karen Magnuson Beil, illustrated by Ted Rand. (1992). New York: Doubleday. There are beautiful illustrations in this tender story of a little girl with a loving grandmother who fits a more traditional view. Grandma bakes the best cookies, has just the right number of "crinkles" (wrinkles), and a lap, as "soft as a pillow."*

Step 2 - Read and Write about the Theme with the Children. The children first discuss each book and then compare them with you. Keep a chart with their comments about the three grandmothers. Later the children can use this chart to write independently about the grandmothers in the story. Which one would you like to have as a grandmother? Write about the grandmother in our story today.

Step 3 - Independent Activities in Centers. Add some activities related to the theme to several of the centers in the room. Here are some suggestions for our Grandmothers and Grandfathers theme.

Reading and Writing Center: Collect a few picture books and other stories about grandmothers and grandfathers from the school or a nearby public library. During the theme study, the children might search the school library for additional books related to the theme, check them out, and put them in the center. Children can write about the grandmothers in the stories you read using the chart developed in Step 2 to help them. They can also write letters or draw pictures to be mailed to a grandparent or grandparents. In case some children do not have a grandparent to write to, keep a list of grandparents who volunteer to be adopted by one of your children as a pen pal.

Math Center: Keep a small collection of pictures of people of various ages. Have the children work alone, or in small groups, to sort the people by how old the children predict they are. Encourage the children to cut out additional pictures from newspapers and magazines you keep for just such an activity. They can make a bulletin board of people sorted by age. Give them some help with the initial categories before you turn them lose on this center, for example, "My Age", "My Teacher's Age", "As Old as Grandparents" to get started. Children can also construct family calendars with birthdays of parents, grandpar-

ents, great-grandparents, and other important family events.

Art Center: The children can draw or paint pictures that remind them of scenes from the grandmother stories you read to them; or, they can illustrate their letters before mailing them.

Discovery Center (science and social studies activities): Many children have grandparents who live far away. Using a simple map of the United States, have children mark where their grandparents live for all to see.

Step 4: Culminating Activity. Plan for a way to end the theme study with the children. Some ways to end our theme unit on Grandmothers and Grandfathers taken from teachers we have observed are listed below:

▌ one teacher brought her grandmother to talk about the teacher as a child and read the teacher's favorite book when she was in kindergarten.

▌ another classroom had children's grandparents volunteer to come to school and read favorite books of theirs to the children and talk about their childhood a long time ago (at least to these five year olds!).

▌ grandparents or adopted grandparents came to demonstrate a special talent in crafts, music, or art (one was a beekeeper!).

▌ one classroom dictated a news item to the teacher, added a photograph of one of their theme activities for a special edition of the school newsletter that was targeted for senior citizens, especially those living in care facilities.

▌ another class took a field trip and were special guests at a senior citizens' weekly meeting at a senior center.

▌ one child's grandfather had an antique car and drove it to the school and children took turns being given rides around the parking lot.

Finally, when playing out a theme, keep it simple in the beginning and follow the children's enthusiasm. Let them keep it alive and growing!

KEEP TRACK OF WHAT YOU DO

Planning

Days come and go very quickly in kindergarten. Planning is important and we recommend you keep a weekly lesson plan book. Use one provided by the school, or go to a teacher supply store, buy one you like, or after looking them all over, make one that suits your needs. Making your own has the advantage of being very flexible, you can change it as you change your teaching style.

Daily Records: So, how did today go? Good question for both the teacher and children to answer. At the end of the day, we suggested as part of your closing routine for each day, take a short dictation chart from the children based on these questions:

▌ What's one thing I learned today?
▌ What are you going to do to get ready for tomorrow?

Getting children to reflect for a few minutes on their day gives them something to think about and to say when someone at home asks, "What did you do today in school?" It also gives you some ideas about what really made an impression, accurate or not, during the day!

You should also reflect on how the day went for you. Once the children are out the door, sit down, put your feet up, get something to drink and jot some notes in a journal or notebook. Start with the same questions you asked the children — did *I* learn anything today? What do I need to get ready for tomorrow? Finally, do a quick check on the whole day's reading and writing activities. Take a look at your plan book and then briefly answer these Yes/No questions:

Did I read to the children today?
Did I model any writing for them today?
Did we read and write together?
Did the children read and write independently today?

These simple questions get at the heart of a kindergarten day in which children see reading and writing modeled for them, participate in shared reading and writing with you and practice on their own. What more could you ask for a successful day!

Informal Checklists

Observing children's reading and writing while it actually happens (Yetta Goodman called this 'kid-watching') is the best way to find out if children are learning. Reporting this information can be useful when talking with parents about their children's progress. The informal assessments in the *Resources* section of this chapter can be used to assess letter name knowledge, concepts about book print, and story sense.

For observations that are a bit more systematic, try Marie Clay's observation tasks in her easy to use *An*

Observe a child's reading and writing as it happens.

Observation Survey of Early Literacy Achievement (1993). Among Clay's observation tasks are letter identification, concepts about print, vocabulary, and writing. The book is well worth the cost and will be useful for many years of teaching.

Portfolios

We present our ideas for using portfolios with kindergarten children in a later chapter of this book. Skip ahead and browse through it any time.

Long Term Evaluation

Daily reflections by you and the children about learning are important. So are longer looks — are children's reading and writing changing and growing over time? How? Do they need more support in learning? What kind of support and guidance do they need? Answering these questions means you will need tools for taking a longer look at children's progress in learning to read and to write. Many schools have elaborate plans for measuring growth and for reporting it to parents. We know you will need to use these plans. However, sometimes they do not tell all or provide enough to guide your daily and long-range planning.

We ran across the checklist in the *Resources* section of this chapter developed by kindergarten teachers and reading specialists in the Tempe (AZ) School District. It breaks children's reading development into three broad stages: Emergent, Early, and Fluency. These areas often overlap, but as you observe children during shared and independent center activities, watch for these skills and strategies. We suggest you watch a few children each week, perhaps one a day and make notes on their reading and writing strengths and needs. Some teachers keep note pads around the room in key places, especially where shared activities take place and centers are located. If you have lots of pockets, stick extra paper in them and get a pen that has a long string you can slip around your neck. Post-it notes are a bit expensive, but some schools will supply them for a teacher to use in taking notes.

Summary

There you have it—one plan for getting through a year of kindergarten. Did we miss something? Probably, but if you start with a sound plan, change it as you and the children learn, and work with other teachers as you share and grow, your children will bloom and bloom and bloom, just like a garden. And, the first grade teacher will bless you a thousand times for sending such a wonderful bouquet of flowering and budding readers and writers to him or her. On to first grade in the next chapter.

Endnotes

1. We are indebted to Jewell and Zintz (1990) and Ann Poole (Tempe, AZ Elementary District) for portions of our descriptions of natural readers and writers.
2. We are indebted to Claire Rottenberg (1993) for her description of Jon's preschool activities.
3. See Resources section of this chapter for articles related to developmentally appropriate instruction.
4. Lev Vygotsky, a Russian psychologist, advocated social interaction as a primary learning tool.
5. We are indebted to Ann Poole, Thew School, Tempe AZ for our ideas about how to use small guided readings with kindergarten children; and to Marie Clay (1991) for her pioneering work in showing teachers how to guide young children's reading.

Resources

Reading List on Developmentally Appropriate Instruction

Reading and Writing Center
    ABC or Alphabet Books
    Number or Counting Books
    Predictable or Pattern Books
    Big Books
Informal Assessments
    Letter Name Knowledge
    Concepts of Book Print Inventory
    Story Sense
Individual Record of Reading Development
    (Kindergarten)

Developmentally Appropriate Instruction

National Association for the Education of Young Children (1988). NAEYC statement on developmentally appropriate practice in the primary grades, serving 5- through 8-year-olds. *Young Children, 43 (2)*, 64-81.

Fields, M. V., Spangler, K. K., & Lee, D. M. (1991). *Let's begin right: Developmentally appropriate beginning literacy.* New York: Merrill.

McIntyre, E. (1995). The struggle for developmentally appropriate literacy instruction. *Journal of Research in Childhood Education, 9*, 145-156.

ABC or Alphabet Books

Alphabet books were originally written to teach children their ABCs, but they have moved beyond that purpose to serve as a showcase for art work or to provide details on specific topics. Here is a sample of some ABC books that you should be able to find in any library:

Mono, M. (1975). *Anno's alphabet.* New York: Crowell.

Bernhard, D. (1993). *Alphabeasts: A hide & seek alphabet book.* New York: Holiday House.

Burningham, J. (1986). *John Burningham's ABC.* New York: Crown Publishers Inc.

Ehlert, L. (1989). *Eating the alphabet.* New York: Harcourt Brace Jovanovich.

Hague, K. (1984). *Alphabears: An ABC book.* New York: Holt, Rinehart, & Winston.

Ipcar, D. Z. (1964). *I love my anteater with an A.* New York: Knopf.

Kitamura, S. (1985). *What's inside? The alphabet book.* New York: Farrar, Straus & Giroux.

Kitchen, B. (1984). *Animal alphabet.* New York: The Dial Press.

Lobel, A. (1981). *On market street.* New York: Greenwillow Books.

Martin, B. & Archambault, J. (1989). *Chicka chicka boom boom.* New York: Simon & Schuster.

Van Allsburg, C. (1987). *The Z was zapped: A play in twenty-six acts.* New York: Houghton Mifflin.

Number or Counting Books

Number or counting books use pictures to help children learn to recognize numbers, count objects, and develop other mathematical concepts. The following number or counting books are favorites of primary teachers:

Aker, S. (1990). *What comes in 2's, 3's, 4's?* New York: Simon and Schuster Books for Young Readers.

Anno, M. (1977). *Anno's counting book* New York: Crowell.

Carle, E. (1968). *1, 2, 3, to the zoo.* New York: Philomel Books.

Cleveland, D. (1978). *April rabbits.* New York: Coward, McCann & Geoghegan.

Crews, D. (1986). *Ten black dots*. New York: Greenwillow Books.

Feelings, M. (1971). *Moja means one: Swahili counting book*. New York: The Dial Press.

Giganti, P. (1992). *Each orange had 8 slices: A counting book*. New York: Greenwillow Books.

Grossman, V. (1991). *Ten little rabbits*. San Francisco: Chronicle Books.

Kitchen, B. (1987). *Animal numbers*. New York: The Dial Press.

Mack, S. (1974). *10 bears in my bed; a goodnight countdown*. New York: Pantheon Books.

Peek, M. (1981). *Roll over! A counting song*. New York: Houghton Mifflin/Clarion Books.

Wadswroth, D. A. (1985). *Over in the meadow: A counting-out rhyme*. New York: Viking Kestrel.

Predictable or Pattern Books

Predictable or pattern books are easy for young children to read because they repeat vocabulary, story language or story structure, or because they use rhythm, rhyme, or familiar sequences like the days of the week. The following are some popular predictable books:

Birmingham, J. (1970). *Mr. Grumpy's outing*. New York: Scholastic Press.

Carle, E. (1984). *The very busy spider*. New York: Philomel Books.

Christelow, E. (1989). *Five little monkeys jumping on the bed*. Clarion Books.

Galdone, P. (1973). *The little red hen*. New York: Scholastic Inc.

Guarino, D. (1989). *Is your mama a llama?* New York: Scholastic Inc.

Hawkins, C. & Hawkins, J. (1985). *I know an old lady who swallowed a fly*. New York: Putnam Publishing Group.

Hutchins, P. (1982). *Goodnight, owl!* New York: Penguin Books.

McLean, A. (1971). *The bus ride*. Glenview, IL: Scott, Foresman.

Sendak, M. (1984). *Where the wild things are*. New York: Harper & Row.

Viorst, J. (1976). *Alexander and the terrible, horrible, no good, very bad day*. New York: Macmillan Publishing Company.

Williams, L. (1986). *The little old lady who was not afraid of anything*. New York: Harper & Row, Publishers.

Wood, A. (1984). *The napping house*. New York: Harcourt Brace Jovanovich.

Big Books

Often ABC books, counting books and predictable books are available in a big book format which allows for group sharing, reading, and rereading. Here are some recommended big books for use in kindergarten classrooms:

Brown, M. W. (1947). *Goodnight moon*. New York: Harper & Row.

Carle, E. (1987). *The very hungry caterpillar*. New York: Scholastic Inc.

Cowley, J. (1987). *Mrs. Wishy-Washy*. San Diego: The Wright Group.

Gelman, R. G. (1987). *More spaghetti I say*. New York: Scholastic Inc.

Hutchins, P. (1987). *Rosie's walk*. New York: Scholastic Inc.

Keats, E. J. (1987). *The snowy day*. New York: Scholastic Inc.

Krauss, R. (1984). *The carrot seed*. New York: Scholastic Inc.

Martin, B. (1982). *Brown bear, brown bear, what do you see?* Toronto: Holt, Rinehart & Winston, Inc.

Numeroff, L. (1985). *If you give a mouse a cookie*. New York: Harper & Row, Publishers.

Sendak. M. (1986). *Chicken soup with rice*. New York: Scholastic Inc.

REFERENCES

Beil, K. M. (1992). *Grandma according to me*. New York: Doubleday.

Clay, M. M. (1991). *Becoming literate: The construction of inner control*. Portsmouth, NH: Heinemann.

Clay, M. M. (1993). *An observation survey of early literacy achievement*. Portsmouth, NH: Heinemann.

Dugan, B. (1992). *Loop the loop*. New York: Greenwillow.

Hoffman, M., & Burroughes, J. (1988). *My grandmother has black hair*. New York: Dial.

Jewell, M. G., & Zintz, M. V. (1990). *Learning to read and write naturally*. (2nd ed.). Dubuque, IA: Kendall/Hunt.

Larrick, N. (1987). Keep a poem in your pocket. In B. E. Cullinan (Ed.), *Children's literature in the reading program* (pp. 20-27). Newark, DE: International Reading Association.

Rottenberg, C. J, & Searfoss, L. W. (1993). How hard-of-hearing and deaf children learn their names. *American Annals of the Deaf, 138*, 358-361.

Searfoss, L. W., & Readence, J. E. (in press). *Helping children learn to read* (4th ed.). Boston: Allyn and Bacon.

Sulzby, E., Branz, C. M., & Buhle, R. (1993). Repeated readings of literature and low socioeconomic status black kindergartners and first graders. *Reading and Writing Quarterly, 9*, 183-196.

A C T I V I T Y

Letter Name Knowledge

Materials: Card printed with upper case letters and second card with lower case letters. Separate form to record responses, use a + sign for correct response, NR for no response, and letter child says if incorrect.

Directions: Hand card with upper case letters to child and say, "Tell me the name of each of the letters I point to." Record responses as you point to individual letters in random order. Repeat this procedure for lower case letters.

Card 1 (UPPER CASE LETTERS)	
A	C
S	W
F	O
K	Y
M	D

Card 2 (lower case letters)	
b	e
h	r
d	n
v	t
s	u

Response Form

Name _____ Date of Screening _____ Grade Level _____

(UPPER CASE LETTERS)		(lower case letters)	
A ____	C ____	b ____	e ____
S ____	W ____	h ____	r ____
F ____	O ____	d ____	n ____
K ____	Y ____	v ____	t ____
M ____	D ____	s ____	u ____

Concepts of Book Print Inventory

Materials: Ask the child to bring to you a favorite book to talk about. Bring several books you think the child might also like, but are unknown to him or her. We use both a known and an unknown book to be certain the child does understand concepts of book print. Have a copy of the checklist below ready to record the child's responses. Use + for correct responses, NR for no response, and record any incorrect responses exactly as said. Add additional questions or comments to the checklist.

Directions: Begin the session by talking about a favorite book you have read and then ask the child to show you the book he or she has brought. Interview the child about the book using the checklist below. Repeat with a book you have brought that is not known to the child. Record all responses on the checklist.

Name _____ Grade _____ Date _____

Child's Favorite Book _____

Teacher's Choice of Unknown Book _____

Interview Statements

Responses

	Favorite Book	Unknown Book
1. Point to the title of the book	_____	_____
2. Show me the beginning of the story.	_____	_____
3. Show me how you read using your finger.	_____	_____
4. Find the end of the story and point to it.	_____	_____
5. (Turn to a page) Show me where we start to read on this page.	_____	_____
6. Show me where the story goes next (after #5.)	_____	_____
7. Find a picture you like.	_____	_____
8. Can you read, or pretend to read, a page in your book?	_____	_____
9. (Read a page in the unknown book). What happened on this page?	_____	_____

(Add additional questions or comments)

ACTIVITY

ACTIVITY

Story Sense

Name _____ Grade _____ Date _____

Materials: Story read or told to the child, or one composed by the child, that has all the elements found in a typical story.

Directions: As the child retells, draws, or writes a story, record the elements found in it.

Name of Story _____

Circle One: Composed Story   Retelling

Type of Retelling   _____ Retelling orally of story read or told to child
(check one)
                     _____ Retelling orally of story from story on tape

                     _____ Retelling used pictures/drawing only

                     _____ Retelling combined pictures/drawings and some written words

                     _____ Written retelling with no pictures of drawings

If the story was an original one composed by the child, what was the inspiration for it? For example, it might be based on a personal experience the child had, another story read or told to the child, or some classroom activities related to a theme.

Recording Story Elements (Use plus sign + for element present and minus sign - for element missing)

_____ Title   _____ Sequence of events (plot)   _____ Character(s)

_____ Feelings or emotions   _____ Time   _____ Setting

Comments or Notes

Individual Record of Reading Development
Kindergarten

Name: _____   Date of entry to school: _____

		SEPT	OCT	NOV	DEC	JAN	FEB	MAR	APR	MAY
BOOK KNOWLEDGE	**EMERGENT 1 - 10**									
	Book: front / back									
	Title / title page									
	Top / bottom of a page									
	Where to begin									
	Left to right / return sweep*									
	Print contains meaning									
PRINT CONCEPTS	Concept of word / space *									
	First / last word									
	1 -1 word match *									
	Differentiate word / letter									
	Identifies high frequency words (min. 10)									
	Identifies some letters									
READING DEVELOPMENT	**EARLY 11 - 13**									
	Takes risks without fear of making errors †									
	Uses picture clues †									
	Reads on to gain meaning †									
	Uses first / last consonant									
	Increases sight vocabulary (min. 40) †									
	Retells story †									
	Identifies periods and question marks									
	Recognizes lower case / capital letters									
	Rereads for meaning †									
	Self corrects †									
	Integrates strategies †									
	FLUENCY 14 - 18									
	Reads with fluency (expression, rate)									
	Silently reads new text independently									
	Identifies quotation marks and commas									
	Integrates cues (meaning, structure, visual graphics)									
	Identifies characters / setting									
	Identifies problem / solution									

These should be mastered before moving to EARLY Level
†*These should be mastered before moving to FLUENCY Level*

ACTIVITY

CHAPTER 5

First Grade
and Beyond

Children who come to first grade from kindergarten come in all sizes and shapes, both physically and in the way they read and write. Some are still emerging as readers and writers, trying to figure out what reading and writing are all about. Others have taken giant first steps, discovered reading and writing, and are racing ahead to develop as readers and writers. Some children have gone beyond those first giant steps and are well on the way to being independent readers and writers—and they know it! The rest of the children fall somewhere in-between. What they all have in common, though, is being in the same classroom with the same teacher who must figure out how to build a classroom where all children can continue to grow and develop as readers and writers.

In this chapter we present our ideas on life beyond kindergarten for emerging readers and writers. We cannot present all the teaching strategies and ideas available to teach reading and writing in grades one and two. We will discuss some basic ideas and suggestions for getting your classroom off to a good start and, as you gain confidence, add in new teaching strategies and your own ideas of how to organize your teaching. The *Resources* section of this chapter lists additional sources for you to use. We will present these topics in this chapter:

▌ Life beyond kindergarten in first and second grade
▌ A plan for organizing and managing the classroom to provide direct instruction and guided practice in skills and strategies
▌ Whole group activities that encourage reading and writing
▌ How to keep track of what you do and ways of assessing children's progress.

LIFE BEYOND KINDERGARTEN

Quite a challenge each year to create a classroom like a big umbrella under which our kindergarten graduates can learn and grow as readers and writers. Let us take a look at the children who come into first grade from kindergarten.

Alex is one of about 15 children in Mrs. Lawson's first-grade class of 28 children who came from kindergarten classrooms in the same building. In fact, over half of these 15 children came from the kindergarten next door. This kindergarten teacher and Mrs. Lawson worked together last year so that these children would have a smooth transition to first grade. These children know Mrs. Lawson by name and are excited because they know of some of the themes they will study and books they will read. In fact, last year some of them even came into Mrs. Lawson's class-

Some first graders are well on their way to reading independently.

room from time to time to read and write with her first graders. They are used to using centers, theme study, and all the kinds of activities described in Chapter 4. Mrs. Lawson has talked with the kindergarten teacher about each child's reading and writing; she knows each one by their first name before the school year begins. Some are already independently reading and writing on, or above, grade level; others are still emerging as readers and writers.

The remaining children are new to the school or district, and some came from families who moved to the district recently. This group also includes children who are independent readers and writers and some who are still emerging; the difference lies in what Mrs. Lawson knows about them. Some have files and some do not; some come from kindergartens similar to the one next door, and others come from very different kindergartens, including half-day or whole-day classrooms.

What do all of these children have in common on this first day of first grade? They are in Mrs. Lawson's room and she has planned a classroom environment for them where they all can bloom as readers and writers. She knows much about some and little about others and has very little time to find out about the new children. She will need the help of the children she knows to be buddies for the new children she does not know.

Mrs. Lawson will need to create a classroom environment that…

▌ encourages children to take risks while producing language—children need to be guided in the skills and strategies of readers and writers and how to use them to learn.

- shares control and decision-making in language learning—sharing control places responsibility on children for learning
- merges instruction and assessment in a seamless web—assessing children by using the products of their reading and writing gives a much better picture of their growth in reading and writing (Searfoss, 1993).

The rest of this chapter is organized around these steps to help you plan and organize your first and second grade classroom.

ORGANIZING AND MANAGING A CLASSROOM

As we mentioned in the kindergarten chapter, it is easy to get bogged down in the details of what you are going to do each day. Before you start doing activities with children, one after the other, we repeat the old saying for you, "Can't see the forest for the trees." Also remember, *you* can read and write, your students cannot—they should work harder than you do! As we thought about how to help you plan your classroom, we made a list of some of the tasks teachers must successfully manage to create:

- arranging the learning environment
- selecting activities and materials to meet students' needs
- grouping children for activities
- managing time schedules
- blending yesterday's activities with today's and tomorrow's
- being flexible when unplanned events occur or the day just does not go the way it is supposed to go.

This list of tasks might seem large and difficult, but with some careful planning we think they all can be accomplished. Here are some suggestions for planning and organizing based on our conversations with teachers, and the work of Jewell and Zintz (1990).

1. *Make a general plan over a period of at least two weeks.* Planning in larger blocks helps you to keep the "forest from the trees." First, write in all "big" or special activities—those which are not part of the regular daily routine, such as visits from older students or volunteers who regularly appear to read to the children. Next, add school-wide events your class is invited to attend and over which you have little scheduling control, along with early dismissals and holidays. Finally, include special activities you have planned

related to a classroom theme under exploration during these two weeks, such as visitors, field trips, and classroom demonstrations. If these are to be a surprise for the students, simply label an activity as a surprise with a question mark. By writing these special activities on a two week calendar, routine activities will not crowd out the bigger activities because you find yourself short of time. Post this two-week calendar where the children, school personnel, parents, and classroom visitors can see it. Figure 5.1 is an example of a two-week schedule of special activities.

2. *Plan daily schedules in larger time blocks.* You can reduce the number of activities in each block, if needed, to prevent trying to squeeze in too much. Remember, not every child needs to participate in everything every day. Larger blocks of time each day make grouping for whole class or small group instruction and activities much easier to do. If you have an aide, volunteer, or student teacher, they can work with a small group or individual student while you work with other children. Larger blocks of time each day are needed for theme study, too, since these activities often take more time to plan and carry out. Figure 5.2 is an example of a daily schedule.

3. *Vary the schedule as needed.* It is hard sometimes to be flexible with 28 children right there, under your nose all day, each day. But, special events that are unplanned (a nice way of saying a disaster or pain in the neck has ruined your daily plan!) can be easier to deal with if you have built in larger blocks of time in your daily schedule. Remember the old saying (oh, no, not another one of those!): "when life gives you lemons, make lemonade." Sometimes children may be

Plan for special activities. Here, storyteller Michale Gabriel engages a child in the story telling process.

Week of _____	A.M.	P.M.
Monday		
Tuesday	10:25 - 10:50 - P.E.	
Wednesday	10:25 - 10:50 - Music	12:30 - 1:00 - Library
Thursday	10:25 - 10:50 - P.E.	1:00 - Early Dismissal
Friday	9:15 - 9:45 - Story Lady	1:00 - 2:15 - Theme Project

Week of _____	A.M.	P.M.
Monday		1:10 - 1:40 Visit gr. 3, 4
Tuesday	10:25 - 10:50 - P.E.	
Wednesday	10:25 - 10:50 - Music	12:30 - 1:00 - Library
Thursday	10:25 - 10:50 - P.E.	
Friday	9:15 - 9: 45 - Story Lady	Grades 1, 2 Assembly?

Figure 5.1. Two-Week Schedule

so involved in an activity you really want them to continue past the scheduled time. An exciting activity related to a theme study might cause more discussion and exploration than planned.

4. *Vary types of activities planned for one day by alternating quieter and noisier ones.* For example, a quiet story reading time might be followed with a movement activity in which a song related to the story is acted out. When children return from recess, a quieter classroom activity can help the day run smoothly. The same advice for the placement of centers. It might be best to have the centers that require physical activity and talking together in one area of the room, away from the quieter reading and writing centers. We will have more to say about centers later in this chapter.

Next we present a daily schedule with some activities in each block of time. Refer to Figure 5.2 as you wade through this discussion—I bet you are hoping we do not say anything more about forests and trees!

Opening Routines and Planning for the Morning

You might want to re-read the section on opening routines in the Kindergarten Chapter. The basic purposes of these opening routines are the same for first and second grades: helping the children to settle into school, feel welcomed in your room, become involved in planning the morning, and having a common language experience. You can begin by having the children take attendance by noting who is not present today using a wall chart with a list of names. A different pair of children can be responsible for this activity each day. Sharing time can begin by recording the news of the day on a large piece of chart paper with

Figure 5.2. Daily Schedule

8:30 - 9:00	Opening Routines	
9:00 - 10:20	<u>Small Groups</u>	<u>Center Time</u>
	Guided Reading Groups (3) Literature Discussion Group (1)	Reading and Library Writing Play and Discovery
10:25 - 11:00	Physical Education	
11:05 - 11:30	Rest and Story Time	
11:30 - 11:45	Individual Activities/Sharing	
11:50 - 12:30	Lunch	
12:45 - 1:00	Planning for Afternoon	
1:00 - 1:15	Sustained Silent Reading	
1:20 - 2:10	Reading Workshops (2 groups)	<u>Center Time</u> Reading and Library Writing
2:10 -2:30	Whole Class—Writing Workshop (Brainstorm topics)	Play and Discovery Projects—(theme)
2:30 - 2:45	Closing Routines	

children giving special news about birthdays or other family events. You can add school news or information and share something of interest. Next, use a large piece of chart paper or a section of a chalkboard to plan the day, noting any special events from the two-week planner posted in the room. Finally, end with a brief language activity such as a story, poem, riddle, or news clipping related to a theme under study or special event.

MORNING BLOCK OF SMALL GROUP AND INDIVIDUAL ACTIVITIES AND INSTRUCTION

In this block of time, children will use the centers and also be part of teacher-directed small group instruction. You can work with groups of four to six for some activities while the remaining children are in centers. First a few ideas about centers, then we will present some suggestions for small group instruction and activities.

CENTERS

First, return to the kindergarten and preschool chapters and review the pages that discuss how to set up and use centers in kindergarten. Some centers can be carried over into first and second grade, especially at the beginning of the year and then phased out and new ones added. In this chapter our centers will be related to reading, writing, and theme study. You can pick and choose among all our suggestions for centers to fit your classroom, and choose which ones you feel are important for your children. Some teachers find the Play and Discovery and Projects Centers we suggest for grades one and two as natural places for social studies, science materials, and hands-on activities to be placed while children are exploring a theme.

Our suggestions for preparing children to use centers independently in the kindergarten chapter apply to first and second graders, too. We discuss these centers for first and second grade classrooms:

> *Reading and Library*
> *Writing*
> *Play and Discovery*
> *Projects*

Reading and Library Center: Books, books, and more books go here. A wide range should be selected beginning with simple alphabet and wordless picture books, predictable and big books, and extending to those chapter books written for third or fourth grade readers. Other kinds of print, too, should be included such as magazines, reference books, 'how-to' and recipe books, and other types of day-to-day print found outside of schools. Books on tape are stored in this center, along with tape recorders and earphones. Children can check out a story tape, recorder, and earphones, and go off on their own to listen to a story. If a small group of children want to hear a story tape, they can move away from this center and find a spot in another place, in or outside of the classroom.

The writing center is a good place for a computer with a simple word processing program.

Writing Center: Placed next to the Reading and Library Center, this center contains all the tools children need to create their own stories, pictures, poems, and other writings. The center should be stocked with a variety of paper including colored construction paper, large and small sheets of plain paper, paper for rough drafts; and plenty of tools such as crayons, markers, pencils, pens, tape, rulers, scissors, paste, yarn, and a small paper punch. A model alphabet, posters with tips for writers, old magazines and other materials with pictures that can be cut out and used to illustrate stories the children create, or books they write, should be present in the center. Book making or binding supplies should also be part of the Writing Center. This center is a good place for a computer with a simple word processing program for children to use. They can create and save their writing and revise later. Stories can be composed and printed, then bound into simple books. Using a computer for these stories removes some of the problems young children often have with making their hand writing easy to read.

Play and Discovery Center: Early in the first grade, some teachers keep the housekeeping center as a part of this center and gradually fade it out. We suggest this center as the place for children to explore and discover collections of materials which may, or may not, be related to themes under study. Social studies, science, and math concepts can be explored through hands-on activities. Oral language development is encouraged as children talk about what they are doing. For example, place one or more magnifying glasses and a collection of objects such as different kinds of fabrics, rocks, plants, or dirt in a box. Show

children how they can explore size, shape, color, and weight of these objects using the magnifying glasses. A simple log or chart of their findings can be kept, with the teacher, volunteer, or the children to record their observations for sharing later with the whole class.

Projects Center: When it needs to be built, glued, painted, or cut out and pasted, this is the center for these type of activities. Materials and supplies of all kinds for all of these "doing" activities should be stored here within easy reach of the children. Covering the floor with a large piece of plastic taped down helps keep the mess under control. Locate this center near a sink or water supply, too, and as far away from other centers as possible so that the noise children make in the center will be less distracting (Jewell & Zintz, 1990). When a particular project is underway related to a classroom theme, step-by-step directions for the children to follow should be discussed with the children and posted in simple words or pictures. For example, in a theme unit on foods, children might make their own restaurant menus, creating a name for their restaurant, and a menu for it. They can list the foods and prices, and draw pictures or decorate the menu by cutting out illustrations from old magazines or restaurant menus.

SMALL GROUP INSTRUCTION AND ACTIVITIES

While some children are working in centers, you can pull four to six of them for small group work that can include:

- Reading and writing workshops
- Literature discussion and response groups
- Reading or writing mini-lessons
- Reading and writing skills and strategies
- Guided reading or writing groups

Reading and Writing Workshops

Reading and writing workshops are a recent approach to teaching reading and writing. If you think of a workshop as a place where things get built using a variety of tools, you have a rough idea of what happens in a reading or writing workshop. Tompkins (1997) lists three key ingredients of workshops:

- Children need large chunks of time to read and to write
- Children should have a choice in what they read or what they write about so they have ownership—*their* books and stories or poems
- Children respond to what they read or write and share it with others

The steps to conducting workshops are simple ones. Workshops can last as long as forty-five to sixty minutes in grades one and two; and can be done in a solid block of time (or at least in the same day, spread across morning and afternoon). A *reading workshop* begins with an introduction to the workshop by the teacher who reads a book to the children; continues with children's self-selected reading of books, perhaps related to a classroom theme, followed by the children responding to what they have read through writing, drawing, or a project; and ending with sharing what they have read with other children. The goal of a reading workshop is for each child to select something to read, read it, respond to it, and then share what they have read. Many ways for children to respond to what they read should be demonstrated for them so they can get beyond the "what I liked about this book" response and go on to drawing, music, or arts and crafts projects.

A writing workshop begins with the teacher modeling, or demonstrating writing, and helping the children brainstorm what they will write about. The process continues with a draft, revising and editing, and ends with children displaying and sharing their writing. Time for peer editing and conferencing with the teacher during the writing workshop is important. Children may want to make a book and illustrate it individually or with other children. The goal of a writing workshop is for the children to complete a full cycle in the process of writing, from brainstorming to producing a final product for sharing.

Some teachers use reading and writing workshops to read and write about a theme under study in the classroom, or teach a mini-lesson on specific skills and strategies as suggested later in this chapter. Workshops are also the time for children to have individual conferences with the teacher about what they are reading and writing. Conferences can be brief and initiated by either the teacher or children. They can focus on ideas or be an opportunity for the teacher to do a quick skills lesson as needed, for example, if a child is having difficulty with beginning sentences with a capital letter. Skills instruction "on the spot" is real to children and likely to be remembered because it is immediately useful to them.

LITERATURE DISCUSSION AND RESPONSE GROUPS

Literature discussion and response groups begin with the teacher and children reading the same whole story or book together. The teacher can read aloud a story in a single session or a longer book broken into parts or chapters across several days. A minimum introduction to the story, using the title and pictures is all that is needed. Other stories can be read silently by the children. If they come to any words they do not know as they read silently, the children should be encouraged to try the unknown word and then ask for help if needed. Literature discussion groups are not the place to stop the flow of reading for a lesson in attacking unknown words. Reading mini-lessons discussed later are the place for these lessons. Once the story or book has been completed, then the children are encouraged to discuss it. The teacher should participate as a reader, too, offering comments and also trying to guide discussion a bit. Until children become familiar with the structure of a literature response group, they may look to the teacher to ask questions or for approval of their reactions to a story. This pattern will fade as they become comfortable with the conversation format of the discussions, where each person can contribute thoughts and ideas freely. A simple way to stimulate discussion, we "borrowed" from a great teacher, is to first get at the story elements and then go on to a deeper discussion. Ask the children to retell the story using the following statements you write on a piece of chart paper:

Somebody in this story....(fill in the character or characters, e.g. *Teresa*)
Wanted... (fill in story line, e.g. *a new bicycle*)
But.....(fill in the problem or challenge, e.g. *her parents would not buy it*)
So...... (fill in how the story was ended, e.g. *Teresa helped her grandmother clean her house for extra money to buy her own bike*)

For the first few literature discussion groups, it is easier to use stories with clear story plots and a few, strong characters children can easily identify.

After reading and orally discussing stories, we suggest you have a follow-up activity children can do on their own while you work with another small group. Children can follow a literature discussion group by re-reading the story alone or with a friend, drawing some illustrations for it, rehearsing it to tell the class or so it can be read to a kindergarten class, reading another book or story on the same theme or by the same author or writing in a response journal. Wollman-Bonilla and Werchadlo (1995) suggested that after children have read and discussed a story, they could be encouraged to write about it using these prompts written on a chart: (1) Feelings I had. Why?; (2) What I liked or did not like; (3) What I wish had happened. Why?; (4) What the book reminds me of. Why?; (5) Questions I have. When children ask if they may write about something not on the chart, tell them they may write whatever they wish about the book or story. Celebrate even the smallest written response to encourage children. You might ask them if they are willing to share their responses with you later so you could read them and write replies.

READING OR WRITING MINI-LESSONS

Reading and writing mini-lessons offer teachers a small group setting for intensive, brief, direct instruction and guided practice in specific skills and strategies. These groups allow the teacher to provide instruction for the different levels of reading and writing abilities in a classroom. Mini-lessons, as Routman (1991) reminds us, are based on calling children's attention to a problem you observe some of them are having in reading and writing. Some teachers observe during reading and writing workshops, and note what skills and strategies might be the focus of a mini-lesson. For example, in a first grade classroom at the beginning of the year, some children may still be struggling with emerging skills such as writing their names, the letters of the alphabet, holding pencils, or story sense. By grouping four to six children together for short instructional groups focused on one skill, the teacher can begin to fill in the gaps in their development as readers and writers. Routman (1991) also cautions us that children do not just "pick up" all the skills they need, and that mini-lessons may need to be repeated again and again for those children who need them.

Roller (1996) lists six components of mini-lessons that follow the direct instruction model:

> Introduction of skill or strategy
> Modeling and explanation
> Feedback
> Guided practice
> Independent practice

Next, we will give you a few examples of mini-lessons or workshops. They can be as simple as these by Roller (1996, page 74) which took five to ten minutes.

Other mini-lessons can be longer and involve more instruction and practice. In one classroom, we observed second graders writing in their journals and noticed that several of them seemed to divide words at the ends of lines without paying attention to syllables. We wondered whether they knew how to divide words and pulled a small group together for a mini-lesson on dividing words into syllables. We gathered a few simple dictionaries and word books from the Reading and Library Center and asked a group of five children who had problems dividing words to bring the stories they were working on to the group.

First, we asked each of them to find a place in their writing where they had divided a word at the end of a line, and wrote these examples on chart paper just as they had been divided by the children. Then we asked the children to explain why they had divided the words as they did. Some could tell us and others were not able to. We quickly moved to having the children work in pairs (we became part of one pair since there were five children) and find the words in a dictionary and compare the spellings there with the ones on the chart. Lots of discussion followed and we finally got a list of corrected spellings. By saying and clapping each word aloud in syllables with the children, they realized that words are divided by syllables at the ends of lines. We then asked the pairs to come up with a rule we could share with the class and add to our list of spelling rules in the Writing Center. After a time, the rule emerged and we printed it on the chart. It went something like: "When you get to the end of a line and need to divide a word, say it out loud and clap the syllables. Divide between the syllables and if you aren't sure, find it in the dictionary." We then had the students revise their stories and apply the rule. Also, several pairs of students volunteered their names for the classroom helpers chart as experts for others to call on when they needed help with dividing words. The whole lesson lasted about 20 minutes.

Minilesson # 1

Introduction:	"Yesterday in class I noticed that when David was reading a book about sharks, he was writing some of the words. I asked him why he was writing the words and he said that it helped him remember them. Writing down words does help some people, and we can use a word bank as a way to organize this writing."
Modeling with explanation:	"There are several ways you can organize your writing and save the words. You can use a notebook, index box, bookmark, or word ring." Show an example of each and explain how it was constructed.
Feedback:	Ask children to summarize why they might want to write down words and how they would go about saving them.

Minilesson #2

Introduction:	"Peter, I noticed that yesterday this word was in your story, 'will.' For most of the story you called that word 'do.' that was fine because the story was making sense. But when you came to the last page you called that word 'will.' It was in the sentence....What happened? How did you know it was 'will' and not 'do?'"
Modeling with explanation:	"Hm. How can you tell this word is 'will' and not 'do?' I'll look at this word and copy it. It starts with a 'w.' 'W' makes a /w/ sound: /w/ /w/ /w/ill. 'Do' starts with /d/, not /w/. So 'will' has to be the right one. I can figure out which word by looking at the beginning sound."
Feedback:	"Is that the way you could tell? By looking at the beginning sound?"

Minilessons. Roller, 1996

READING AND WRITING SKILLS AND STRATEGIES

What skills and strategies should you teach in first and second grade? There are many sources that list the skills and strategies often taught in first and second grade, often in a rough sequence. Often each school district and state has mandated skills and strategy lists to help you. Commercial materials you purchase will also suggest what to teach. Some schools and commercial materials provide informal tests throughout the year to help you decided what skills and strategies children have learned and still need to learn. All of these lists are useful in helping you keep track of what you have taught to which students. We do not want to present one list of skills for you to follow. As you gain experience teaching, the task of deciding which ones are important becomes easier. The best rule we know to follow is one we suggested earlier: *If you cannot demonstrate the value of the skill directly to children (or if you have to use an answer key), it probably is not worth teaching.* So, whether it is a...

...phonics skill such as initial consonant sounds
...comprehension skill such as sensing sequence of events in a story
...study skill such as using parts of a book or a simple dictionary
...new vocabulary word
...spelling rule or tip
...writing mechanics skills such as when to use a question mark

Be certain the skill or strategy is really worthwhile and can be applied directly by the children to their daily reading and writing. Your teaching will be easier and the children's learning more rewarding. Next, we need to say a word about *phonics* and how it is useful to beginning readers and writers.

We believe that teaching children a strategy such as figuring out the meaning of an unknown word requires a organized pattern of skills that also should be taught. For example, in teaching children to use the unknown word strategy we discussed in the kindergarten chapter, there are several underlying skills

Teach a strategy for figuring out an unknown word.

children need to have in if they are to be successful in applying this strategy. Remember the strategy?

What Do You Do When You Get Stuck
Go back. Try again.
Use the pictures.
Point to the word.
Get your mouth ready and try to sound it out.
Does it make sense?
Were you right?

When children are asked to "get your mouth ready and try to sound it out," there are some phonic skills we assume they have to be successful. But, teaching children phonics skills, no matter how well it is done, also assumes children have had the necessary practice with language to profit from phonics instruction. One kindergarten teacher we observed said, "They've got to have some language sense." To find out what she meant, we observed in her classroom, and generated a list of behaviors her successful phonic learners had: they listened to stories read to them or on tape, were interested in writing, created their own personal or invented spellings for words, and played with words in all kinds of rhyming and other word games.

Researchers also have tried to help us understand that children who are successful readers and writers develop *phonemic awareness*, or the ability to use the relationship between letters and the sounds they make. Phonemic awareness means understanding that letters have names and matching sounds. It also means that children can sense, or are aware of patterns or sound units in words (e.g. top, hop, stop), and can pull apart these sound units and patterns as they make new words (e.g. m + op = mop). Phonemic awareness lays a strong foundation for later formal, direct phonics instruction. Tompkins (1997), listed in the *Resources*

section of this chapter, has an excellent discussion of phonemic awareness with many teaching activities.

GUIDED READING AND WRITING PROCESS GROUPS

The purpose of reading or writing process groups is to demonstrate and model a process for the children and provide them guided practice. Many children coming into first and second grade still needing this process instruction.

Guided Reading

We introduced you to guided reading in the kindergarten chapter as a way of teachers guiding children through the process of reading a whole book or story at one time, and for children to practice their oral fluency and reading strategies. As they move into first and second grades, some children become very independent and need little formal guided reading. They can move into literature discussion and response groups very easily. There are still many children who are emerging as readers and need the structure of guided reading to help them succeed. The steps in guided reading were explained in detail in the kindergarten chapter, beginning on page 41. Return to that section and review them. The only major difference when using guided reading in first or second grades is in the difficulty and length of the books or stories used. Choose stories where more of the plot is carried by the words and less by the pictures as children's reading fluency improves.

Guided Writing

Guided writing is similar in purpose to guided reading—we try to demonstrate to small groups of children what is involved in the writing process and how they can complete a piece of writing from beginning to end under our guidance. We model writing a poem, for example, and guide them through the steps to producing one of their own as a small group.

WHOLE GROUP ACTIVITIES THAT ENCOURAGE READING AND WRITING

Encouraging and providing time to practice reading and writing is a major part of any classroom reading program. Sometimes the whole class can be involved in reading and writing. Whole group or class reading and writing activities should be a regular part of your school day. Here are a few suggestions for whole class or group activities that teachers have found useful over the years.

Sustained Silent Reading

Sustained Silent Reading or SSR (sometimes called DROP—Drop Everything and Read) provides time for the children and the teacher to read on their own something they have selected. The children get time to practice reading for fun and the teacher serves as a role model for reading. The peer pressure of being surrounded by readers is a powerful tool for getting reluctant readers to settle down and read. Searfoss and Readence (1994, p. 37-8) explain the rules of SSR.

SSR, or Sustained Silent Reading. Once called USSR (uninterrupted, sustained, silent reading), SSR has been around for a number of years. It was originally intended to provide everyone, including the teacher, with a quiet time to read. With everyone in the classroom reading at the same time, both peer pressure and the modeling effect serve to help children increase and sustain their independent reading for increasingly longer periods of time. Over the years, many variations of the SSR rules have been suggested:

1. Don't try to sell SSR to the whole school. First graders and sixth graders require different amounts of SSR time, and even a different time of day for scheduling SSR. Also, individual teachers will want to schedule SSR to fit individual classroom schedules and programs. The authors strongly urge that children be involved in the planning and scheduling of SSR times and in the amount of time given to SSR.
2. Discuss SSR with the children, and post your interpretation of the rules. Tierney, Readence, and Dishner (1990) present three cardinal rules of SSR:

   Everybody reads.
   There are no interruptions during SSR.
   No one will be asked to report what he or she has read.

   Use a kitchen timer instead of the classroom clock to signal the beginning and end of the SSR period. Remember: you, the teacher, are a model fluent reader for your children. If you spend the SSR time glancing back and forth from the clock to what you are reading, this is hardly good modeling.
3. Read with your class. SSR is not "shut up and read" time, so take some time to relax with a favorite piece of writing and enjoy it. Try a novel,

a professional book, a new children's book, poetry, the newspaper—but be sure to select something for your pleasure reading.
4. Start SSR with the phrase "Does everyone have something to read?" Avoid saying "a book to read," since that implies that only books are good enough for SSR.
5. Adjust the SSR time to fit your children, gradually increasing it. Beginning with 5 minutes and moving slowly to 20 or 25 minutes is the general pattern.
6. Be consistent and follow the rules. Handle fidgeters and disruptive children quickly and without lectures on proper behavior. Simply inviting yourself to sit next to a potentially disruptive child often has a calming influence in a hurry. If only a few children are fidgeters, see that they place themselves out of the line of sight of the others. Make them comfortable near you or in their own little corner.

SSR can provide an excellent opportunity for children to silently practice reading. It is simple, cheap, and easy to implement and keep going. A last word on SSR: Keep the students involved in planning the SSR daily time period and the length of the period and also in finding ways to be certain that everyone has a chance to read, quietly and without interruptions.

Alarm Clock Reading. The purpose of alarm clock reading is to give some direction and structure to children's at-home reading. The exact steps in the technique, suggested originally by Greene (1970a), are certainly adaptable. The important element of alarm clock reading is the regular recording children do as they read each day at home. This recording is crucial to starting a habit of reading independently at home. The basic steps are these:

1. Select an easy book to read for alarm clock reading.
2. Set a stove timer or alarm clock so that it will ring 15 minutes after you begin to read.
3. Read your book as rapidly as you can until the alarm rings.
4. After the alarm rings, count the number of pages (to the nearest half page) and record it somewhere. Keep your daily log in a place where you can find it.
5. Close your book, and tell yourself out loud what you just read.
6. Do alarm clock reading each day, and keep your record up to date.

Log format will vary by the grade level of the children. Whatever the form, space should be provided for recording daily progress, as shown below.

```
Book Title: _____
Number of Pages: Mon. _____  Tues. _____
                 Wed. _____   Thurs. _____
                 Fri. _____   Sat. _____
                 Sun. _____
```

Some parents keep the log sheet on the refrigerator door. If children have a special place to study, a log can be tacked to a small bulletin board. Weekly logs can be transferred to a reading folder in school, so that the teacher can review the log with each child. Some teachers might wish to develop a log format with simple drawings, duplicate it, and provide it for children to get alarm clock reading started. Later, children might design their own logs. Some children will already be reading regularly at home and may find alarm clock reading unnecessary. Teachers can suggest they continue with their independent reading and not use an alarm clock reading log. The authors have found, though, that these children adjust to almost any system of recording their at-home reading, since it is already a habit for them.

Sustained Writing Time

Sustained Writing Time (SWT) is exactly what the term says—a time for the children and the teacher to write without interruptions. As with SSR, the teacher serves as a role model and peer pressure gently nudges reluctant writers to write. Also, as with SSR, the choice of what to write should be the children's choice. You can suggest some ideas, such as writing in a journal or learning log, finishing some piece of writing started earlier, or copying a favorite poem, riddle or joke. We will discuss journals and learning logs a bit more.

Journals

The teachers we talk with have different opinions about journals; some say they are a wonderful tool for writing and encouraging self-expression by children, and other teachers tell us they take too much time, and some children just will not write in journals. We believe, for young children in grades one and two, journal writing can be encouraged and successful if the children see a clear reason or purpose for writing. *Response journals* are really more like letters two people exchange on a regular basis about what

they are reading. It is natural for children to talk about what they are reading, to express feelings and opinions about a story or book. In many classrooms, teachers just simply cannot get around to listening to every child's talk about reading. By encouraging the children to write their responses in a journal, you offer them a place to be heard when your ears are busy; and, a place for you to write a reaction to their responses. The response journal allows the children to write to you as they read a book or story and gives you time to respond to it later.

With first and second graders, keep the journals simple. Wollman-Bonilla (1991), in her small, easy-to-read book on response journals, suggests they can be introduced to children first by modeling or demonstrating what they are:

> *One of the best ways to communicate what response journals are is to show students a sample first. The response you share may be your own, or one written by a student in another class. Choose a response that reflects at least some of the range of possibilities inherent in journal writing, or compose a sample response. Preferably it should be a response to a text students know. Write an honest response that reflects what you thought as you read (p. 21).*

Do not worry about how much the children write at first, the important connection you want them to make is that writing is one very natural way to respond to reading. Keep children's responses in a journal format so each writing session is added to the previous one. After a time, children will collect a journal that can become part of their writing portfolio and look back at all the responses they made throughout the year.

Learning Logs

While response journals are places where children respond to stories or books, *learning logs* allow a place for children to react to what they are learning in school. A learning log written at the end of the day might include answers to these questions:

1. *What is something you learned today about _____?* (insert a word from social studies, math, science, or from a theme under study)
2. *What do you do to get ready for tomorrow?* (e.g. homework, bring something from home)

Learning logs can be modeled first as group experience charts at the end of the day by the teacher and whole group. As the children offer ideas, the teacher

Read to children every day – nothing is more important!

writes them on the chart and talks about them with the students. As writing becomes easier for them, children can switch to individual learning logs or add a section to their response journals each day with answers to the two questions. Done regularly, learning logs lay a strong foundation for good study habits and give children something to say when someone at home says, "What did you learn today in school!"

Read Aloud and Story Telling Time

Reading to children and telling them stories is one of the most rewarding and satisfying activities teachers do. We suggest you read books or tell children's stories that *you* find interesting. Read those books and stories by children's authors that are your favorites. Do not worry, the children will not miss that classic you hate—let someone else read it to them! There are no special instructions or talent you need to read to children, they are the best audience we know and will forgive almost anything. Besides, you have the only copy of the story in front of you, how would they know if you skip words or certain parts of a story? Just read to them every day, every day, every day—and we mean every day, nothing you do is more important.

Telling stories sometimes makes people nervous. Somehow storytelling has become organized in this country and we now pay people money to come and tell us stories. Again, relax, all you need to tell a good story is a story you like and want to tell, a few oral practice sessions ahead of time and you are ready to go. If a story or book is too long for one session, read parts and tell parts of it, or spread the telling out over several days. We always hear the voice of Nancy Larrick (1987), who always has a poem in her pocket, reminding us to share a poem, too, at least several

times a week as an alternative to story telling. Not the poems some of us had to memorize in our school days (or was it daze?), but today's children's poets such as Jack Prelutsky, Myna Cohn Livingston and so many others.

Theme Study

We have already presented several thematic units in the preschool and kindergarten chapters. They were simple theme units nestled in and around other classroom activities. Some teachers try to base much of their daily teaching around broad themes that often last for a week or more; other teachers prefer the short-burst theme unit with a much narrower focus. That is a personal choice you can make. Some themes are teacher's choices or part of an established school curriculum you are expected to follow. We urge you to be certain to include a theme study now and then that comes from the children and the experiences they are having in your classroom. A special classroom visitor, holiday, community or school event, or current news story can be the trigger for a wonderful theme study, pulled together quickly and much less organized than more formal thematic units. Centers can be changed to reflect a theme, with the children helping you. Remember, you already know how to read and to write, give the children the practice in helping change center activities and materials.

Thompson (1991) and other writers generally suggest these steps for getting a theme study off the ground and completed with a minimum amount of chaos:

1. Introduce the theme and have the children brainstorm ideas about it. Share a poem, song, or story related to the theme with the children; perhaps one of them can do the same. Have the children respond to the song or story with some small group activities.
2. Read about the theme in all kinds of print and if you have a computer, use the Internet to search for information. Collect all kinds of sources of information and books about the theme and place them in the Reading Center.
3. Help the children plan individual, small group, or a whole class project related to the theme.
4. Plan for a sharing time for the projects or share with other classrooms, parents, or anyone willing to sit still and listen.

How to Keep Track of What You Do and Assessing Children's Progress

Planning

Just like kindergarten, days come and go very quickly and we suggest you use some kind of lesson plan book. Buy one at a teacher supply store, use the one the school may provide for you, or create your own using a computer software program.

Daily Records

Refer back to the kindergarten chapter, beginning on page 41, for our suggestions on how to keep records of how your days go. This type of reflection on what worked, did not work and what you would do differently tomorrow is the most important part of planning and assessment.

Informal Checklists

Some experts believe that checklists restrict your thinking rather than encourage it. We prefer to use checklists as a place to organize your observations about children; and, we change them as needed. Frankly, with 25 - 30 children to keep track of, we find checklists a convenient way to keep records of children's progress for later use in parent conferences and in completing report cards. See the *Resources* section of this chapter for some informal reading checklists used by one school district in first and second grade. Use them "as is" or change them to meet your needs. Marie Clay's text, *An observation survey of early literacy achievement* (1993), is another good source of informal reading and writing assessment. One assessment tool Clay finds very useful is running records. We cannot present all there is to know about running records, but here is a brief overview of how to use this simple technique.

Running records, as explained by Clay, are recordings of how children read orally. Have children read orally, one at a time, a short selection from a story they are currently reading in your classroom. The texts used for Guided Reading, explained in the kindergarten chapter, are often used to record a running record. We refer you to Clay's book for a thorough explanation of running records. You can get started, though, by using the following simplified directions:

1. Find a text the child has already read. Later use a text not known to the child to see how he or she applies strategies to a new story; but for your first experiences use stories the children know.
2. Ask the child to read orally a part of a story no longer than 100 words. Record what the child says on a blank sheet of paper. Use a check mark (✓) for each correct word; record errors exactly as the child read. There are several marking systems used; what is important is that you to be able to go back and reconstruct what the child said at a later time. We suggest tape recording your early tries at taking running records so you can play the tape back and check your markings. We use this system for recording what a child says:

Says correct words:

Text: The sky was blue.

Child: ✓ ✓ ✓ ✓.

Substitutes one word or part of a word for what is written:

Text: The dog ate my shoe!
Child: ✓ ✓ ✓ ✓ shirt/shoe

Inserts a word or words:

Text: The sun was hot and so was Dusty.
Child: ✓✓✓✓✓∧ ✓✓✓. (he was)

Self-corrects with attempts:

Text: The sun was hot and so was Dusty.
Child: ✓✓✓∧ ✓ ✓✓. (he was SC)

Repeats word or words (*not counted as error*):

Text: The sun was hot and so was Dusty.
Child: ✓✓✓ hot ✓✓✓✓. (↩)

Asks for help:

Text: The sun was hot and so was Dusty.
Child: ✓✓✓✓✓✓✓Ⓐ

No response—child hesitates but does not attempt word or words:

Text: The sun was hot and so was Dusty.
Child: ✓✓✓✓✓✓/Dusty. (NR)

Omits a word or words:

Text: The sun was hot and so was Dusty.
Child: ✓✓✓✓ (and) ✓✓✓.

4. When the child finishes the passage, sit back and analyze the error rate:

1:5 or less (one word wrong in every five)	Text too difficult
1:10	Text can be read with help
1:20	Easy reading text

5. Finally, analyze the kinds of errors and whether they are significant or not by asking these questions suggested by Searfoss and Readence (1994):

Text: The horse jumped over the gate.
Child: The horse jumped over the fence.

Is the reading making sense?

Is the reading grammatically correct?

Does the child make use of visual cues in letters and words?

Running records are a quick snapshot of what happens when a child reads orally. Be certain to have the child return to what has been read to find out if comprehension is there. A simple retelling of the story will do. Running records are supposed to be a quick on-the-spot way to monitor children's reading growth. Once you have done them for a few weeks, you will find them easy to administer. The more your read about them, the more useful they can be.

Long Term Evaluation

Portfolios. We present our ideas for developing and using portfolios in a later chapter. Skip ahead and browse through it any time.

Assessing Children's Progress

The *Resources* section of this chapter contains several checklists for assessing what children are learning over time. These checklists, from one school district, may be used as part of Guided Reading to assess progress as children move from emerging readers, to early reading, to fluent reading in grades one and two. We thank the teachers and staff in Tempe (AZ) School District for sharing them with us.

Assessing Classroom Environments

The second checklist in the *Resources* section, Assessing the Literacy Environment (Searfoss, 1993), should be used to assess the organization and use of resources in your classroom. Adapt it to your needs, but we urge you to step back and take a look at your classroom environment three or four times a year. Some teachers self-assess their own classrooms using the checklist and then ask at least one fellow teacher to serve as an outside assessor. By comparing notes, a teacher can get both an insider's view and an outsider's view of the classroom environment.

Summary

Well, we have come to the end of the chapter on how to help first and second graders bloom as readers and writers. Is there life beyond kindergarten? Yes, there certainly is. Children will continue to grow as readers and writers in first and second grade if your classroom offers them a combination of direct instruction, lots of practice in reading and writing, and many opportunities for developing independence. We hope you have grown as a teacher and as a reader and writer, too, as you read our ideas for your classroom in this chapter.

RESOURCES

Clay, M. (1993). *An observation survey of early literacy achievement*. Portsmouth, NH: Heinemann.
    Observation techniques for classroom teachers to use in assessing oral language, concepts about print, and early reading skills and strategies.
Glazer, S., & Brown, C. (1993). *Portfolios and beyond: Collaborative assessment in reading and writing*. Norwood, MA: Christopher-Gordon.
    The authors have collected a treasury of classroom assessment techniques here for teachers to use. Chapters on assessing writing and comprehension are especially useful.
Hagertry, P. (1992). *Readers' workshop*. New York: Scholastic, Inc.
    Practical suggestions and mini-lessons to help teachers set up readers' workshops.
Jewell, M. G., & Zintz, M. A. (1990). *Learning to read and write naturally* (2nd ed.). Dubuque, IA: Kendall/Hunt.
    The authors have written a book full of wonderful ideas for teachers and worth mining for all that is there. Good sections on reading and writing activities in the primary grades.

Peterson, R., & Eeds, M. (1990). *Grand conversations: Literature groups in action.* New York: Scholatic, Inc.
"The" book on understanding and doing literature discussion or response groups.

Roller, C. (1996). *Variability not disability: Struggling readers in a workshop classroom.* Newark, DE: International Reading Association.
Describes how to use readers' and writers' workshops, provide direct instruction, and create a simple record-keeping system based on teachers' observations.

Routman, R. (1991) *Invitations: Changing teachers and learners K-12.* Portsmouth, NH: Heinemann.
Few authors are better at putting the specifics of how to teach beginning readers and writers. Routman creates classrooms where 'real' reading and writing, and skills and strategies all seem to come together. Sample the chapters on beginning reading, writing, and assessment for ideas in the book. You will not be disappointed.

Tompkins, G. (1997). *Literacy for the 21st century: A balanced approach.* Upper Saddle River, NJ: Merrill/Prentice Hall.
Nice, thick book full of wonderful ideas on how to teach reading and writing. The author really speaks to teachers in this text, clearly and with practical ideas. Use as a reference and thumb through the index for topics of interest. Good section on phonemic awareness.

Thompson, G. (1991). *Teaching through themes.* New York: Scholastic, Inc.
Practical, step-by-step guide to theme teaching. Includes sample theme studies.

Wollman-Bonilla, J., & Werchadlo, B. (1995). Literaure response journals in a first grade classroom. *Language Arts, 72,* 562-570.
Writing and reading come together in response journals for first graders in this article that shows teachers how to encourage a wide range of responses to literature.

Wollman-Bonilla, J. (1991). *Response journals.* New York: Scholastic, Inc.
Suggestions for getting response journals started across the curriculum.

REFERENCES

Clay, M. M. (1993). *An observation survey of early literacy achievement.* Portsmouth, NH: Heinemann.

Jewell, M. G., & Zintz, M. V. (1990). *Learning to read and write naturally* (2nd ed.). Dubuque, IA: Kendall/Hunt.

Larrick, N. (1987). Keep a poem in your pocket. In B. E. Cullinan (Ed.), *Children's literature in the reading program* (pp. 20-27). Newark, DE: International Reading Association.

Roller, C. M. (1996). *Variability not disability: Struggling readers in a workshop classroom.* Newark, DE: International Reading Association.

Routman, R. (1991). *Invitations: Changing teachers and learners K-12.* Portsmouth, NH: Heinemann.

Searfoss, L. W. (1993). Assessing classroom environments. In S. M. Glazer & C. S. Brown (Eds.), *Portfolios and beyond: Collaborative assessment in reading and writing* (pp. 11-26). Norwood, MA: Christopher-Gordon.

Searfoss, L. W., & Readence, J. E. (1994). *Helping children learn to read* (3rd ed.). Boston: Allyn and Bacon.

Thompson, G. (1991). *Teaching through themes.* New York: Scholastic.

Tompkins, G. E. (1997). *Literacy for the 21st century: A balanced approach.* Upper Saddle River, NJ: Merrill/Prentice Hall.

Wollman-Bonilla, J. E. (1991). *Response journals: Inviting students to think and write about literature.* New York: Scholastic.

Wollman-Bonilla, J. E., & Werchadlo, B. (1995). Literature response journals in a first-grade classroom. *Language Arts, 72,* 562-570.

Class Record of Reading Development Grade One (enter date when student progresses to the next stage) List Names	EMERGENT 1-10	Book: front / back	Title / title page	Top / bottom of a page	Where to begin	Left to right / return sweep *	Print contains meaning *	Concept of word / space *	First / last word	1-1 word match *	Differentiate word / letter	Identifies high freq. words (min. 10)*	Identifies some letters	EARLY 11 - 13	Takes risks without fear of making errors †	Uses picture clues †	Reads on to gain meaning †	Uses first / last consonant	Increases sight vocabulary (min. 40) †	Retells story †	Identifies periods and question marks	Recognizes lower case / capital letters	Rereads for meaning †	Self corrects †	Integrates strategies †	FLUENCY 14-18	Reads with fluency (expression, rate)	Silently reads new text independently	Identifies quotation marks and commas	Integrates strategies (meaning, structure, visual graphics)	Identifies characters / setting	Identifies problem / solution

These should be mastered before moving to EARLY level. † These should be mastered before moving to FLUENCY level.

A C T I V I T Y

Individual Record of Reading Development
Grade One

Name: _____ Date of entry to school: _____

EMERGENT 1 - 10	SEPT	OCT	NOV	DEC	JAN	FEB	MAR	APR	MAY
Book: front / back									
Title / title page									
Top / bottom of a page									
Where to begin									
Left to right / return sweep*									
Print contains meaning									
Concept of word / space *									
First / last word									
1 - 1 word match *									
Differentiate word / letter									
Identifies high frequency words (min. 10)									
Identifies some letters									
EARLY 11 - 13									
Takes risks without fear of making errors †									
Uses picture clues †									
Reads on to gain meaning †									
Uses first / last consonant									
Increases sight vocabulary (min. 40) †									
Retells story †									
Identifies periods and question marks									
Recognizes lower case / capital letters									
Rereads for meaning †									
Self corrects †									
Integrates strategies †									
FLUENCY 14 - 18									
Reads with fluency (expression, rate)									
Silently reads new text independently									
Identifies quotation marks and commas									
Integrates cues (meaning, structure, visual graphics)									
Identifies characters / setting									
Identifies problem / solution									

These should be mastered before moving to EARLY Level
† These should be mastered before moving to FLUENCY Level

Guided Reading for *Early Level* Readers

DEFINITION: The early reader is developing independence by integrating strategies to gain meaning from print.

Natural Language Texts: Levels 11 - 13   Basal: Primer Level and beyond

The reading levels apply to K-1 typically, but the following teaching procedure should be used with students at any grade level who are not consistently using strategies.

PRE-PLANNING

▌ Identify students' **Instructional** reading level (90-94% on Running Record) and select appropriate book/story.

▌ Preview book/story to determine teaching strategies to be used in Guided Reading lesson.

▌ Focus on a skill and a few unknown high frequency words for instruction in context. This information can be obtained from Record of Reading Development form, Running Records, and monitoring information.

TEACHING PROCEDURE

Step 1   Tell title and brief main idea. Talk through the story looking at the pictures asking students to predict. It is important to ask open-ended questions. Leave opportunities for students to use strategies.

Step 2   Pose questions relating to story. Tell the students to silently read the first page or pages. Ask for the answer to the questions then have a student read the answer orally to confirm.

Step 3   Briefly introduce 1 - 2 teaching points (not each page). Reinforce teaching points and high frequency words from previous lessons. Discuss the story to foster comprehension.

Step 4   Read together providing a fluency model. The student should read without pointing during this fluency practice.

Step 5   **After reading the story, running records should be taken on one or two students. Ask students to retell the story.**

Step 6   Students take the book home to read to parents. Teacher places returned book in book basket for further independent practice.

INDEPENDENT PRACTICE

Provide opportunities throughout the day for students to read from a selection of books at an independent level. These books should include both seen and unseen texts.

EVALUATION

Each student will demonstrate the behaviors listed:

* Take risks without fear of making errors
* Reads on to gain meaning
* Increases sight vocabulary to a minimum of 40
   Identifies periods, question, exclamation marks
* Rereads for meaning

* Integrates strategies
* Uses picture clues
   Uses first / last consonant
* Retells story
   Recognizes lower case / capital letters
* Self corrects

These should be mastered before moving to the fluency level.

The word "ACTIVITY" appears vertically in the left margin.

Guided Reading for *Emergent Level* Readers

DEFINITION: The emergent reader is developing print concepts and learning that the text and illustration tell a story. They often memorize the text.

Natural Language Texts: Levels 1 - 10   Basal: Pre-Primer[1] - Pre-primer[3]

The reading levels apply to K-1 typically. The teaching procedure should be used with emergent readers at any grade level.

PRE-PLANNING

❚ Identify students' instructional reading level (90-94% on Running Record) and select appropriate book/story.

❚ Preview book/story to determine teaching strategies to be used in Guided Reading lesson.

❚ Focus on a skill and an unknown high frequency word for instruction in context. This information can be obtained from Record of Reading Development form, Running Records, and monitoring information.

TEACHING PROCEDURE

Step 1   Tell title and brief main idea. Talk through the story looking at the pictures asking students to predict. It is important to ask open-ended questions. Leave opportunities for students to use strategies.

Step 2   Read the text together pointing to the words. Reinforce what to do when you come to an unknown word. Refer to pictures as clues to establish *meaning*.

Step 3   Read the story together stopping briefly for appropriate teaching point. Discuss the story to foster comprehension.

Step 4   Read together with teacher providing a fluent model. If possible, the student should read without pointing during this fluency practice.

Step 5   Students read the story independently. **Running records should be taken on one or two students at this time. Have the students retell the story after the running record.**

Step 6   Students take the book home to read to parents. Teacher may want to listen to students read individually the next day. Teacher places book in book basket for further independent practice.

INDEPENDENT PRACTICE

Provide opportunities throughout the day for students to read from a selection of books at their independent level. These will be books previously introduced [seen text] in the reading group (example: book baskets, news journals, big books, poetry cards).

EVALUATION

Each student will demonstrate the behaviors listed:

Book: front/back	Title/title page
Top/bottom of a page	Where to begin
Left to right/return sweep	* Print contains meaning
* Concept of word/space	First/last word
* 1 - 1 word match	Differentiate word/letter
* Identifies minimum of 20 high frequency words (Fry's High Frequency Word List)	Identifies some letters

These should be mastered before moving to the early *level.*

ACTIVITY

Guided Reading for *Fluency Level* Readers

DEFINITION: The fluency level reader is achieving independence by integrating meaning, structure and visual graphics to comprehend more complex text. This should include a variety or genre in fiction and non-fiction.

Natural Language Texts: Levels 14 and beyond   Basal: Level[12] and beyond

For students who are having difficulty reading, teachers could use the emergent or early level procedures until students are more proficient.

PRE-PLANNING

▌ Identify students' instructional reading level (90-94% on Running Record) and select appropriate book/story.

▌ Preview story to determine teaching strategies to be used in Guided Reading lesson.

▌ Identify focus skill for instruction in context. This information can be obtained from Record of Reading Development form, Running Records, and monitoring information.

TEACHING PROCEDURE

Step 1   Introduce the book with a short book talk to the reading group. **Take a running record on one or two students while the rest of the group is silently reading.**

Step 2   Discussion between teacher and students:
▌ Establish comprehension (story structure)
▌ Teaching points
▌ Vocabulary, etc.

Step 3   Students take home an *unseen* text at their instructional level.

INDEPENDENT PRACTICE

Provide opportunities throughout the day for students to read from a selection of books at their independent and instructional levels. These books should include seen and unseen texts, which will provide opportunities for students to do independent problem solving.

EVALUATION

The student will demonstrate the behaviors listed:

Reads with fluency (expression, rate)
Silently reads new text independently
Integrates cues (meaning, structure, visual graphics)
Applies knowledge of literary elements
Understands punctuation

CHAPTER 6

Inclusion: Literacy Development for All Children

Young children are remarkably accepting of differences if they are presented to them directly and simply. It is important to help children understand differences rather than pretend we are all the same. As you will read next in Cory's classroom, acknowledging differences is the first step toward true acceptance of them in classrooms.

CORY'S INCLUSION CLASSROOM[1]

"A mother once came to me before school started," Cory told us, "concerned that the other children in kindergarten would make fun of her daughter's turned in eye. Rather than telling the group about how it would be cruel to mention Aubrie's difference, we talked about how we all had eyes, how our eyes were different colors and shapes, and Aubrie herself brought up how hers were different in another way. The children asked Aubrie what it was like and whether or not she could see and how things looked. It was never brought up again."

What happens, though, when the difference is much greater than Aubrie's? Cory told us she was concerned when Tommy, in a wheelchair, joined her kindergarten classroom. She worried about meeting Tommy's needs, while at the same time Cory wondered if she would have enough time and energy for the needs of the other children in her room. At first Cory's room was not wheelchair accessible from outside the building; a short ramp built by the district carpenters fixed that easily. In the classroom, chairs and tables were separated a bit more to allow space for Tommy to wheel around the room by himself. At first, Cory assigned a peer pal to Tommy to help him learn about the rules and schedules of the school and the classroom. Gradually, as Tommy made friends, Cory stopped that practice. Tommy really did not need someone assigned to him; he made friends and they all helped each other when needed. Cory could not keep track of the job descriptions of the different people who came into her classroom to work with Tommy. Out of frustration, she decided everyone working with Tommy would be called a teacher. His aide was there not only to help Tommy, but she was another teacher for *all* of the children. By making certain Tommy's aide did not spend all of her time one-to-one with Tommy, the aide became part of the classroom team.

WHAT IS INCLUSION?

Inclusion is really a simple idea. It means children with disabilities are not to be educated in separate programs and classrooms, far away from the regular, daily life of most children in a school. While Public

A child's aide should become part of the whole classroom.

Law 94-142, section 612, the first law requiring children with disabilities to be included in regular classrooms, was passed over 20 years ago, many schools are still struggling with making inclusion a reality. The original law, strengthened by the Americans with Disabilities Act of 1990, calls for schools to educate children with disabilities in regular classrooms, side-by-side, with children who do not have disabilities. Special classes for children with disabilities are allowed by law only when the disability is so severe that a child will not learn in a regular classroom, even if it is modified for his or her special needs. Schools are also required to include the parents of disabled children in the development of individual educational plans (IEPs) for their children.

All children in regular classrooms benefit where children with disabilities are included (see Freagon, S. et al, 1995; Staub & Peck, 1994/1995). Children with disabilities gain opportunities to choose friends to play with and to model behaviors of non-disabled children. All children learn to accept and appreciate how we are alike and different, to be thoughtful and caring, as they become less afraid of human differences.

The placement of children with disabilities in regular classrooms, however, does not necessarily guarantee benefits in every classroom. The most important ingredients for successful inclusion are the ability, knowledge, and attitude of the teacher (Zionts & Baker, 1997). Teachers are the most creative, flexible, adaptable people on this planet—they have to be able to work in schools where space, time, and resources are often in short supply. Many teachers, though, do not have the experience, or the training, they feel they need to work with children who have disabilities. We found, however, that most of the teachers we talked to who worked in inclusion classrooms did not have a special list of language teaching strategies or a special curriculum for children with disabilities or special needs. Most of the changes in their classrooms were to modify the physical environment or daily schedules to accommodate children with disabilities rather than the major changes in the curriculum.

The rest of this chapter presents some ways to manage and organize classrooms and suggest some resources useful to teachers as they try to include all kinds of children in regular classrooms. The *Resources* section of the chapter contains a list of suggested readings on creating inclusive classrooms. Browse the list, select a source or two, and try some of the ideas the authors suggest.

ORGANIZING AND MANAGING INCLUSION LEARNING ENVIRONMENTS

In his article on the curriculum in an inclusion classroom, Cambone (1994) suggests that teachers can improve the learning of disabled and emotionally troubled children by managing their teaching through three simple changes in classroom life. While Cambone's article focused on children with social problems, we feel his suggestions are useful for all inclusion classrooms.

1. *Predictable schedules.* To be successful, inclusive classrooms, from the first day of school, need clear and predictable schedules that do not change greatly from day-to-day. Posting the daily schedule and reviewing it two or three times during the day with the children also contribute to making learning successful. Notice Cambone said "predictable," not "rigid"; if the schedule needs to be changed, then children can be prepared for the change before it happens. Discussing changes and how to make them with the children involves them in making decisions in the classroom.

2. *Transitions.* It is important to plan time between activities so children can "cool down" from one activity and move to another. A short discussion about the transition from one activity to another saves lots of time repeating directions and directing traffic in the classroom for children who seem to be confused about where to go and what to do.

3. *Rules for responsibility.* Classrooms need to be based on a clear social contract based on rules and responsibilities for behavior. Making rules, and the consequences for not following rules, clear to children is important, of course, but, it does not teach them how to be responsible for their own actions. Rewarding appropriate behaviors is a great idea—we all like to be praised and given a reward for doing well. Making children's responsibilities clear, such as doing homework, getting supplies, and picking up after an activity, is very important for all children, but especially for disabled children. They should be held to the same standards of social conduct and manners as the non-disabled children as much as possible.

Also, children should be involved in planning daily schedules. Smith and Misra (1992) offer some good ideas for negotiating schedules with children through discussion. Children should take over writing and posting the daily schedule after the teacher has discussed the day's activities with them. For very young children at the very beginning stages of writing, a group experience chart dictated to the teacher will accomplish the same purpose. Alternating activities between those that require lots of work and thinking with those that are easier, keeps attention spans from wandering. Make sure students know what to do when they finish a task early. Posting a list of suggestions under the heading, "When you finish, then you may_____," helps build independence and responsibility. Finally, make certain parents know the daily schedule, understand classroom rules, and are kept informed about their children's responsibilities.

Getting disabled children to become part of the social life of the classroom is a very important part of inclusion. Teachers tell us about how concerned they are that friendships develop among all children in their classrooms. Since children naturally want to be friends and have friends, the next section of this chapter talks about how teachers can encourage friendships and other social contacts in inclusion classrooms.

DEVELOPING FRIENDSHIPS IN INCLUSION CLASSROOMS

As we read about friendships and how to help children get along in inclusion classrooms, an article by

Bergen (1993) describes what can happen if teachers and children try too hard to accept a child with a disability. Bergen warns in her article that sometimes children with disabilities run the risk of becoming classroom "pets." Some children may act like "mother hens" toward the disabled child, robbing the child of the chance to be independent even in small tasks such as getting supplies or moving about the room. All the teachers we talked with, and the children in their classrooms, were a bit worried about how they would react when a child with a disability was about to come into their classroom. They all wanted to be sure the new member of their classroom felt welcomed and part of the classroom. They did not want their children to feel sorry for the new member of the class.

Exploring the meaning of friendship and how to be a friend are ways of helping non-disabled children develop healthy relationships with disabled children. Here are some ways to help children build friendships:

1. Create a class scrapbook that includes samples of writing, art, or other projects from everyone in the class. The scrapbook can relate to a theme under study, holiday, or other class events.
2. Build a class wall mural by having each child complete a part of the mural.
3. Draw and decorate a class tree. Each branch of the tree can include a picture of a child or a sample of writing, art, or other project.
4. Publish a class "Who's Who" book. Children can each have a page in the book to tell something about themselves, their interests, achievements, or family. A picture of each child should also be on the page.
5. Design a "We're Proud of" bulletin board with the children. They can post their work on the board.
6. Take some time each week for a "Spotlight Time" where the whole class acknowledges special achievements or accomplishments of individual children, in and out of school.
7. Publish a class newspaper with each child getting a turn writing or illustrating a news item. Children can also write and illustrate items for the newspaper in pairs or small groups. Children with special interests can become regular columnists for an issue or two in areas such as sports, community and school news, or letters to the editor.
8. Use recess or gym time and a "nerf" ball for a friendship activity. Tell the children that they are going to talk about friendships. Each time one of them catches the ball when you throw it, they have to call out what makes a friend. Once the game is underway, children can take over throwing the ball, too.
9. Read or tell a story from the *Bibliography of Children's Books about Inclusion* in the *Resources* section of this chapter and have the children respond to the story. You might want to turn to Chapter 5 and review the literature response and discussion activities. Learning and talking about differences seems easier when it is done through a good story.
10. Create a simple friendship chart or poster based on what a friend sounds like or looks like and post it in the class. Here's a sample:

HOW TO BE A KIND FRIEND

A KIND FRIEND SOUNDS LIKE:	*A KIND FRIEND LOOKS LIKE:*
Please and thank you.	*Shaking hands.*
Do you want to play?	*Playing together.*
That's good.	*Helping people up.*
I like you.	*Smiling together.*
Sorry.	*Sitting together.*
Will you be my friend?	*Helping clean up.*

Helping children learn how to make friends and keep them is an important part of growing and learning. While you will not find friendship as a tested skill on achievement tests, children with friends seem to enjoy learning and school much more than children who have trouble forming friendships. So, tested on or not, plan on including friendship building in your classroom curriculum.

Summary

Deciding to offer children with disabilities the opportunity to be included in regular classrooms is not only a legal requirement in our public schools; it is simply the right thing to do, with or without laws. If teachers get the kind of support they need to learn how to organize and manage an inclusive classroom, everyone benefits. We hope this chapter starts you on the road to learning more about inclusion classrooms. The *Resources* section is a good place to go to learn more about inclusion, beginning with the *References for Teachers' Self-Study about Inclusion*.

Endnotes

1. We thank Cory Hansen for her descriptions of how she included children with disabilities in her kindergarten classroom.

RESOURCES

References for Teachers' Self-Study about Inclusion
Bibliography of Children's Books about Inclusion

REFERENCES FOR TEACHERS' SELF-STUDY ABOUT INCLUSION

Bergen, D. (1993). Facilitating friendship development in inclusion classrooms. *Childhood Education, 69*, 243, 246.

Cambone, J. (1994). Braided curriculum in the inclusive classroom. *Journal of Emotional and Behavioral Problems, 3*, 41-44.

Eichinger, J., & Woltman, S. (1993). Integration strategies for learners with severe multiple disabilities. *Teaching Exceptional Children*, 18-21.

Freagon, S. (1995). Inclusion of young learners with disabilities in social studies. *Social Studies and the Young Learner, 7*. 15-18.

Friend, M., & Cook, L. (1992). Helping teachers manage the inclusive classroom. *Instructor, 101*, 30-32, 34, 36.

Putnam, J. W. (1993). *Cooperative learning and strategies for inclusion.* MD: Paul H. Brookes.

Raynes M. (1991). A fresh look at categorical programs for children with special needs. *Phi Delta Kappan, 73*, 326-331.

Sardo-Brown, D., & Hinson, S. (1995). Classroom teachers' perceptions of the implementation and effects of full inclusion. *ERS Spectrum, 13*, 18-24.

Stainback, S., & Stainback, W. (1992). Including students with severe disabilities in the regular classroom curriculum. *Preventing School Failure, 37*, 26-30.

Staub, D., & Peck, C. A. (1994/95). What are the outcomes for nondisabled students? *Educational Leadership, 52*, 36-40.

Van Dyke, R., Stallings, M. A., & Colley, K. (1995). How to build an inclusive school community: A success story. *Phi Delta Kappan, 76*, 475-479.

Wheeler, J. J. (1991). Educating students with severe disabilities in general education settings: A resource manual.

Whittaker, C., (1996). Adapting cooperative learning structures for mainstreamed students. *Reading & Writing Quarterly, 12*, 23-39.

Zionts, P. (1997). *Inclusion strategies for students with learning and behavior problems: Perspectives. experiences and best practices.* Austin, TX: Pro-ed.

Bibliography of Children's Books about Inclusion

Read these books to children or tell them as a story to them. Follow with a discussion of the book and how it made them think about differences, or a specific disability, and what they learned.

Books about Differences

Brown, T. (1984). *Someone special just like you.* New York: Holt.

Bunting, E. (1994). *Smoky night.* San Diego: Harcourt Brace.

Kellogg, S. (1989). *Is your mama a llama?* New York: Scholastic.

Kraus, R. (1971). *Leo the late bloomer.* New York: Windmill.

Morris, A. (1990). *Loving.* (Photographs by Ken Heyman). New York: Lothrop, Lee & Shepard.

Visual Impairment

Cohen, M. (1983). *See you tomorrow, Charles.* New York: Greenwillow Books.

Hermann, H. (1988). *Jenny's magic wand.* Chicago: A. Whitman.

McConnell, N. P. (1983). *Different and alike.* Colorado Springs, CO: Current.

Newth, P. (1981). *Roly goes exploring.* New York: J. P. Putnam.

Rosenberg, M. B. (1983). *My friend Leslie: The story of a handicapped child.* New York: Lothrop, Lee & Shepard Books.

Sargent, S., & Wirt, D. A. (1983). *My favorite place.* Nashville: Abingdon.

Yolen, J. (1977). *The seeing stick.* New York: Crowell.

Cerebral Palsy

Payne, S. N. (1982). *The contest.* Minneapolis, MN: Carolrhoda Books.

Whinston, J. L. (1989). *I'm Joshua and "yes I can".* New York: Vantage Press.

Cystic Fibrosis

Arnold, K. (1983). *Anna joins in.* Nashville, TN: Abingdon.

Hearing Impairment

Ancona, G., & Miller, M. B. (1989). *Handtalk zoo.* New York: Four Winds Press.

Aseltine, L., Mueller, E., & Tait, N. (1986). *I'm deaf and it's okay.* Niles, IL: A. Whitman & Co.

Charlip, R., Miller, M. B., & Ancona, G. (1980). *Handtalk: An ABC of finger spelling and sign language.* New York: Four Winds Press.

Charlip, R., Miller, M. B., & Ancona, G. (1987). *Handtalk birthday: A number and story book in sign language.* New York: Four Winds Press.

Fain, K. (1993). *Handsigns: A sign language alphabet.* New York: Scholastic.

Greenberg, J. E. (1985). *What is the sign for friend?* New York: F. Watts.

Peterson, J. W. (1977). *I have a sister: My sister is deaf.* New York: Harper & Row.

Rankin, L. (1991). *The handmade alphabet.* New York: Dial Books.

Zelonky, J. (1980). *I can't always hear you.* Milwaukee, WI: Raintree Publishers.

Down's Syndrome

Cairo, S. (1985). *Our brother has Down's syndrome: An introduction for children.* Toronto: Annick Press.

Shalom, D. B. (1984). *Special kids make special friends.* Bellmore: Association for Children with Down's Syndrome.

Physical Impairment

Caselesy, J. (1991). *Harry and Willy and Carrothead*. New York: Greenwillow Books.

Donovan, P. (1982). *Carol Johnston: The one armed gymnast*. Chicago: Children's Press.

Kaufman, C., & Kaufman, G. (1985). *Rejesh*. New York: Atheneum.

Nadas, B. P. (1975). *Danny's song*. Northbrook, IL: Hubbard.

Wolf, B. (1974). *Don't feel sorry for Paul*. Philadelphia, PA: Lippincott.

Physical Impairment - Wheelchair

Fassler, J. (1975). *Howie helps himself*. Chicago: A. Whitman.

Greenfield, E. (1980). *Darlene*. New York: Routledge, Chapman & Hall.

Marron, C.A. (1983). *No trouble for grandpa*. Milwaukee, WI: Raintree Publishers.

Muldoon, K. M. (1989). *Princess Pooh*. Niles, IL: A. Whitman.

Rabe, B. (1981). *The balancing girl*. New York: Dutton.

Raffi. (1988). *One light one sun*. New York: Crown Publishers.

Seuling, B. (1986). *I'm not so different*. Racine, WI: Western Publishing.

REFERENCES

Bergen, D. (1993). Facilitating friendship development in inclusion classroom. *Childhood Education, 69*, 243-246.

Cambone, J. (1994). Braided curriculum in the inclusive classroom. *Journal of Emotional and Behavioral Problems, 3*, 41-44.

Freagon, S. (1995). Inclusion of young learners with disabilities in social studies. *Social Studies and the Young Learner, 7*, 15-18.

Smith, M. A., & Misra, A. (1992). A comprehensive management system for students in regular classrooms. *The Elementary School Journal, 92*, 354-371.

Staub, D., & Peck, C. A. (1994/1995). What are the outcomes for non-disabled students? *Educational Leadership, 52*, 36-40.

Zionts, L., & Baker, P. (1997). Inclusion and diversity: Powerful words with powerful meaning. In Zionts, P., *Inclusion strategies for students with learning and behavior problems: Perspectives, experiences and best practices* (pp. 339-367). Austin, TX: Pro-ed.

CHAPTER 7

Assessing Early Literacy through Portfolios

Introduction

In our society, it seems as though we all are always being tested, poked, evaluated, and assessed from birth until the end of our lives (Glazer & Brown, 1993). Daily in day care, preschool, and elementary schools information is gathered about children. We seem to want to know how our children are doing, just to be sure all is well and they are developing normally. In this chapter we present a simple, natural way, to organize in one place all the information we gather on children's progress in learning to read and write by using *portfolios*. This chapter presents a definition and description of a portfolio, what it can be used for, and how to construct one.

AMY'S PARENT CONFERENCE

Amy is in Ms. Harris' first grade classroom. Ms. Harris and the children in her room have invited parents to an evening of "Look What I Can Do" as a way of showing parents what their children are learning. Ms. Harris has reserved the library for this special occasion and the children have decorated it with displays of their favorite books and their own writings. As the parents arrive with their children, Ms. Harris greets them and offers them something to drink and some cookies. Amy takes her parents and her portfolio, with its colorful cover full of pictures she has drawn, to a small table and chairs. She shares what is in her portfolio and why she included each item. Amy reads a story she wrote about two animal friends that are separated from each other by a river. They cannot play with each other until they figure out a way to get across the water. Amy tells of many ways that the friends try to cross the river. Finally, they are successful and hug each other once again. Amy also illustrated the story. Her parents ask questions about the story and other work they find in Amy's portfolio. Ms. Harris allows Amy to explain what has been included and why. At the end of the conference, Ms. Harris talks with Amy and her parents about the progress Amy has made as a reader and a writer. She shows Amy's parents a log of what Amy has read so far this year, with Amy's favorites circled. Ms. Harris picks two writing samples, one from earlier in the year and a recent one and shows Amy and her parents how much growth there has been in Amy's writing skills. The conference ends with Amy and her teacher listing two or three goals for Amy to work on before the next conference.

Ms. Harris, Amy, and her parents made good use of a portfolio. Amy helped select what was in the portfolio, Ms. Harris added a few things, and the work was used to show her parents the progress Amy has

made. Most importantly, it is Amy's portfolio and she led the conference. Amy feels in charge of her learning and is able to talk about it with her parents. Using portfolios as part of parent conferences is just one use for portfolios.

What is a Portfolio?

By now you may have figured out that a portfolio, like the kind Amy used in her classroom, is really samples of her work that are kept in one place and tell us about her reading and writing skills, interests, and how these change over time. It is work Amy is proud of and wants to share. The term, "portfolio," is borrowed from the art world where an artist's portfolio is a sample of his or her best work for clients to see. For those who know a bit about investing money, a person's portfolio contains a list of all the different kinds of investments someone might have such as stocks, bonds, IRA's, and others. So, a portfolio is a collection, whether it is of Amy's work, an artist's paintings, or someone's investments. It is personal and different for each child in the classroom.

GETTING PORTFOLIOS STARTED

If you ever doubted the need for a portfolio of each child's work, think about all the products of reading and writing children create, the formal and informal tests they take, and all the other written records of their progress. A portfolio makes sense as a simple way to organize and display their work. But, how much work does it take to construct a portfolio? Do you save everything? Here are some questions you need to think about and answer before you begin using portfolios:

1. *What will the portfolios be used for?* If they will be used mainly for conferences with parents, as in Amy's classroom, then a portfolio will contain lots of samples of children's writing, records of what they have read, projects, and other products from the reading and writing centers in your room. If we want to use the portfolios to assess a child's progress and as a source of information for writing comments on report cards, then adding math work and other samples from unit or center activities in science and social studies is appropriate. In some schools, the portfolio *is* the report card. You might want to include any tests the child has been given, especially if they are school or district required tests. *What goes in a portfolio should be determined by what you are going to use it for.* It is not a place to put everything a child gener-

ates. Remember it is not like a garage, attic, or storage shed full of stuff we just could not throw away! If a portfolio is crammed full of stuff and not organized, it will not be useful for much of anything.

2. *Who will put things into the portfolio?* Once you know what you are going to use the portfolio for, then it becomes easier to figure out who will contribute to it. Naturally, children and teachers will contribute. You might want parents, volunteers, classroom aides, or student teachers also to add items to the portfolio. We suggest starting portfolios with a few children at a time and gradually adding several children each week until all the children have started portfolios.

3. *How will the children know what to do with their portfolios?* You will need to demonstrate to the children what a portfolio is and how it will be used. You might construct a portfolio from one child's work for a few weeks and use it in your demonstration, with the child helping you tell how you both added to it. Or, you could use some portfolios from previous classes you have taught. Perhaps a child from last year's class could come and give a demonstration of how to build a portfolio and what it is used for.

4. *Where will we keep the portfolios?* Locate a space for storing and organizing the class portfolios. Mark it for portfolios only with a label or sign. Some teachers place the portfolios and materials needed to make them in a special portfolio center until the children get used to adding to it. As one teacher said, "I remind the children that portfolios are like gerbils, they need to be fed and watered regularly!" Once portfolios become part of the regular routine of the classroom, then it is no longer necessary to keep them as a formal center. They can be moved to a small space in the room. In other classrooms we have seen portfolios become part of reading and writing centers so it is easier for children to get into the routine of adding the products of reading and writing to their portfolios.

5. *What do portfolios look like?* The physical portfolio is often an accordion-type or expandable folder with pockets for children's work. Each pocket is used for a particular kind of work, for example, all writing samples would go into one pocket and a written log of books read into another, along with any written comments about books. Teachers and children often make their own portfolios from cereal or other kinds of boxes. A portfolio can also be made by stapling construction paper together along one side to create a portfolio. The outside of the

portfolio can be personalized with a label and drawing by each child or with a photograph of the child.

6. *Finally, what goes into a portfolio?* A child's portfolio reflects the activities going on in the classroom. As you review the activities in our preschool, kindergarten, and grades one and beyond chapters in this text, you can see what kinds of work we mean. Here are some suggestions we gathered from teachers who use portfolios. You might want to start your own list, a small one a first, and gradually add to it, as you become more familiar with portfolios.

Portfolio Contents

1. Samples of student's work selected by the student, teacher, or the student with teacher guidance.
   a) samples from writings (e.g., The shark is swimming in the water. The shark came on land. Everybody ran away. By Sacha, age 5).
   b) audiotapes of storytelling or show and tell reporting
   c) photos of projects or experiments
   d) drawings of stories
   e) drawings, collages
   f) creative self-expression projects
   g) lists of written words
   h) videotapes of projects
2. Teacher observations.
   a) anecdotal observation records
   For example:
   2/28/97 Nikki has had fun with our Valentine's day activities. She has shared her Valentines with her friends.
   2/28/97 Tyler has really been enjoying our transportation theme. He acted out what it would be like to be a motorcycle.
   b) checklists (inventories including lists of behaviors or skills for students to achieve, developmental, criterion referenced, teacher developed)
3. Student's own periodic self evaluations reported by teacher
   a) interest inventories (e.g. questions may include: Do you have a hobby? If so, what is your hobby? What is your favorite book? What is your favorite story that your parent reads to you. What is your favorite movie? What is your favorite story? What do you like to do after school? What is your favorite food/toy?)
   b) (e.g. questions may include: How do you feel about going to school? How do you feel

about reading books? How do you feel about writing stories? How do you feel about your teacher? How do you feel about drawing?)

4. Progress notes contributed by the student and teacher collectively.
5. Log books (vocabulary growth, books listened to and told to the class or new projects)
6. Criterion Referenced tests
7. Parent observation (parents should be invited to make observations of their child's literacy interests and pursuits, for example: Natasha's brother Mikhail read *Miss Nelson is Missing* (1977) to the whole family. Natasha drew a picture detailing the story.)
8. Parent-Teacher conferences (summaries or reports)
9. Parent-Teacher communications (lists and descriptions of telephone conversations, brief discussions, notes, reports and etc.)
10. Goals

In the rest of this chapter, we want to talk about another use for portfolios—brief, individual conferences you might have with each child.

USING PORTFOLIOS FOR INDIVIDUAL CONFERENCES

Portfolios are a great way to talk with children about their progress and growth in reading and writing. You can establish a regular schedule of conferences with children, say two or three a day, and post a schedule so the children can get ready for their conferences. Some teachers have children sign up for individual conferences whenever the children are ready, gently reminding reluctant children now and then that it is time for a conference with you. Try to meet each child at least once a month, depending on how many children you are responsible for. Your first conference will require more time than later ones, but once a routine is established conferences should be brief, often as short as two or three minutes, and no longer than five or six minutes (Gelfer & Perkins, 1992; 1991).

Children should get ready for their conferences by making certain their portfolios are up-to-date. Encourage them not to sign up for a conference unless they are ready for one. For children in grades one and beyond, some teachers have the children do a practice conference with a friend before signing up with the teacher.

During these individual conferences, stress the positive changes you see at the beginning of each conference. For example, you might comment on a child's latest story having a good title and a beginning,

middle, and an end. You might compare it with an earlier story so the child can see progress in mechanics such as handwriting or punctuation. After you have talked about positive changes, set one or two small goals with the child for the next conference, such as spacing more carefully between words or reading an additional book before the next conference. These goals can be written down for older children to review in the portfolio. For younger children, they can be talked about. Children should leave a conference knowing they have made some progress and with a goal or two to work on.

The *Resources* section of this chapter contains some sample guide sheets and other forms for use with portfolios. They are only suggestions and you should change them to fit your children and needs. Feel free to use them however you wish, including ignoring them when you have a better suggestion!

Summary

Portfolios can help you and your children organize their work so you can both talk about the progress they have made and set some goals for the future. Portfolios can also be used to talk with parents and other caregivers about the children's progress in learning to read and write. Children must be actively involved in building their own portfolios and in keeping them up-to-date. Yes, they do require some time and planning, but we think the rewards are worth the investment. Begin slowly, and gradually portfolios will become a valuable part of your teaching and your children's learning.

RESOURCES

This section contains sample guide sheets, forms to use with portfolio conferences, and some sample progress reports.

Sample	Title
1	Getting Started—Guide Sheet for First Conference
2	Reading and Writing Inventory
3	Attitude Survey About Reading
4	Reading Record
5	Setting Goals: Activity Sheet
6	Book Review Sheet
7	Greetings: MY PORTFOLIO
8	Sample Progress Reports for Use with Portfolios

Have a conference with each child to praise and offer new goals.

——— S A M P L E ———

#1: Getting Started—Guide Sheet for Initial Portfolio Conference

Name _____ Date _____

The following questions can be used as part of the first portfolio conference with children.

Reading
Do you have someone to read to you at home? Who?
Do you like people to read to you?
What kinds of stories do you like best? funny, happy, make believe, scary.
Do you have any favorite story characters? Tell me about them.
Do you know someone who likes to read? Why do they like to read?
What do you like to read?

Writing
Do you like to write?
Do you like to draw pictures about stories and books?
Do you know someone who is a good writer? What makes them a good writer?
What do you like to write about?

──────── S A M P L E ────────

#2: Reading and Writing Inventory

Student _____ Date _____

To get a sense of student's attitude toward reading and writing, ask:

1. Are you a good reader? Why or why not?
2. Are you a good writer? Why or why not?
3. Do you like to read? Why or why not?
4. Do you like to write? Why or why not?
5. Do you read or write at home? What?

To gain a sense of student's interests ask:

6. Tell me about your favorite book.
7. What are your favorite things to do?
8. Do you have any hobbies?
9. What person would you like to be?
10. Who is the most interesting person you know?

Recognition of student's control of reading and writing strategies, ask:

11. How do you decide what to read?
12. How do you decide what to write?
13. Do you like to guess what is going to happen when you are reading a story?
14. When you read do you see pictures in your mind? How does that work?
15. If things are not going well when you are reading and writing, what do you do?

──────── S A M P L E ────────

#3: Attitude Survey About Reading

Name _____ Date _____

Carefully read each statement. Then for each one make a T for True and an F for False.

1. _____ I do not like to read.
2. _____ I am scared to read aloud.
3. _____ I feel very good when I finish reading a book or story.
4. _____ I like to read quietly to myself.
5. _____ Sometimes I cannot remember everything I read in a story.
6. _____ Sometimes I do not want to read because I am bored.
7. _____ I skip words do not know.
8. _____ Keeping a reading log is not fun.
9. _____ If I like a book I will try to find other books that are written by the same author.
10. _____ I like my teacher reading books aloud in the class.
11. _____ I do not like reading books with the print too small.
12. _____ I think 20 minutes is too long to read at one time.
13. _____ I like reading aloud.
14. _____ I enjoy reading in a group with children who read at the same speed as I do.
15. _____ I enjoy telling my classmates about a book I liked reading.

─── S A M P L E ───

#4: Reading Record

Name _____ School Year _____

Book Title   Author   Started   Finished

_____

_____

_____

_____

─── S A M P L E ───

#5: Setting Goals: Activity Sheet

Directions: At the beginning of the year, provide your children with a list of goals that are appropriate and are easily recognizable. Then have each one select from the list a few goals they would like to learn. After each conference include additional goals, if identified goals are being met.

Name: _____

Date: _____

These are some things I would like to learn this year.

_____

_____

Date: _____

_____

_____

Date: _____

_____

_____

──────── S A M P L E ────────

#6: Book Review Sheet

Directions: After reading each book, children may dictate information to you or complete the review sheet independently.

Name _____ Date _____

Title of Book _____
Author _____
Illustrator _____

How did you enjoy the book? Circle your answer:

How did you enjoy the drawings?

Would you read the book again?

What did you enjoy most about this book?

What did you enjoy least about the book?

──────── S A M P L E ────────

#7: Greetings: My Portfolio
(could be used at each conference)

My name is _____

I go to school at _____

My teacher's name is _____

Today's date _____

(Students can verbally answer these questions and the teacher can record the responses)

How is my portfolio organized _____

What does my portfolio show about me _____

What does my portfolio show about my reading _____

What does my portfolio show about my writing _____

What does my portfolio show about my math _____

_____ S A M P L E _____

#8: Progress Reports for Use with Portfolios

A. Our Progress

Name of student: _____

Teacher's name: _____

Date of this report: _____

Strengths	Teacher Reflections	Student Reflections

Should Work On	Teacher Reflections	Student Reflections

B. Progress Report

Student: _____

Date: _____

For the portfolio collected between _____ and _____

Problem Solving: _____

_____

_____

Literacy and Language: _____

_____

_____

Creative Expression: _____

_____

_____

C. Teacher Checklist for Student's Ability to Retell a Story

Student's Name _____

Title and Author of Book _____

	1	2	3
Includes information directly in the text.			
Includes inferred information in the text			
Includes a summary or synthesizes			
Reflects on the information			
Asks additional questions			

D. Student-Teacher Conferencing Checklist

Student's Name _____

Date _____

_____ When writing in my journal I can do the following:

_____ I write about things that interest me.

_____ I write stories about real things, people, places.

_____ I write make-believe stories.

_____ I illustrate my stories.

_____ I put periods, question marks, and exclamation marks at the end of the sentence.

_____ I start each sentence with a capital letter.

_____ I make the people in my stories speak.

_____ I use new words in my stories.

Other things I do when I write my stories.

E. Portfolio Evaluation

Student: _____

For the portfolio collected between _____ and _____

	Reading			Writing	
Advancing	Moderate	Minimum	Advancing	Moderate	Minimum

Comments:

	Attitudes of Reading			Interests in Reading	
Hot	Neutral	Cold	Hot	Neutral	Cold

Comments:

	Progress as a Reader			Progress as a Writer	
Excellent	Observable	Limited	Excellent	Observable	Limited

Comments:

REFERENCES

Gelfer, J. I., & Perkins, P. G. (1991). Teacher-parent partnerships: Enhancing communications. *Childhood Education, 67,* 164-167.

Gelfer, J. I., & Perkins, P. G. (1992). Constructing student portfolios: A process and product that fosters commu-

nication with families. *Day Care and Early Education, 20,* 9-13.

Glazer, S. M., & Brown, C. S. (1993). *Portfolios and beyond: Collaborative assessment in reading and writing.* Norwood, MA: Christopher-Gordon.

CHAPTER 8

Second Language
Learners

Sophia sits next to Maria and watches her friend write a letter to her grandmother. Each time Maria writes, so does Sophia on her piece of paper. They both giggle and laugh as they scribble and draw a message. This familiar scene is repeated thousands of times each day in preschools and elementary-school classrooms all over the country. Two children, emerging as writers and friends, share their writing with each other. As you get closer to these two, your ears will perk up. Maria is chattering away in Spanish and English to Sophia; Sophia is nodding her head, giggling with her face full of interest in what Maria is saying. Sophia says few words, for she speaks only rarely in English since she arrived from Russia a few months ago. Maria and her family, however, have lived in the same neighborhood near the school for several generations and she has learned to live in a world of English and Spanish, quite comfortably.

Children in our country who speak a second language, other than English, are increasing in numbers each year, no matter what source you read. By the year 2000, the number of second language learners in our schools is expected to reach between 3,000,000 and 4,000,000 and by the year 2020 greater than 6,000,000. In some states, the increase in the number of these students is astounding and schools often struggle to teach them to read and to write. In fact, a large majority of teachers report they have little or no training in how to work with second language learners (see Gersten, 1996; Spangenber-Urbschat & Pritchard, 1994). Also, there are many terms applied to these children. *We prefer to use the term second language learner to define a student who is learning English as a second language, or ESL learner for short.*

Children who come to day care centers, preschools, and elementary schools with a language other than English have such a wonderful gift not shared by those of us who have only mastered one language. Sometimes, however, children with two (or more) languages are viewed negatively and labeled as children with learning problems simply because they have two languages. This attitude, that second language learners are handicapped or deficient in some way, is sad. We have observed teachers who resort to talking louder and slower in English, while struggling to help ESL learners, as if these children were hearing-impaired or less gifted with brain power. The message some ESL learners hear is, "there is something wrong with me." In many parts of the world, however, having two languages is not only a necessity for survival and communication, it is encouraged.

Teaching second language learners to read and write along with children who only speak English is a challenge for teachers at all levels, not because of the children as much as other factors. *First,* many teachers and caregivers are not prepared to work with

Teaching second language learners along with children who only speak English is a challenge.

second language learners, as we mentioned earlier. *Second,* for those of us who only speak English, communicating with second language learners can be frustrating when children do not understand what you say. *Third,* in addition to a language other than English, ESL learners, especially recent immigrants like Sophia, often come from cultures that are very different than mainstream America. *Fourth,* there is much diversity in both background of experiences and in native language fluency among ESL learners. An ESL learner whose family recently moved from Taiwan so his parents could accept employment as engineers with a microcomputer company here in the United States, and the ESL learner whose parents were driven from their country by poverty and war are two different learners. The first child may have had excellent opportunities to learn to read and write in formal schooling, while the second learner's major concerns were more basic—safety, food, and shelter. *Fifth,* when mixed with larger numbers of children who speak English, time to work with second language learners just seems difficult to find without extra hands or helpers. *Finally,* many experts agree that it often takes years for children to learn conversational English and be comfortable with it and even longer to be able to learn through content materials such as textbooks used in schools.

What we hope to do in this chapter is to give you some practical suggestions for working with second language learners. We also want to relieve some of your anxiety about the teaching strategies that we are suggesting. There are, in fact, few ESL teaching strategies that do not make sense for *all* kids. Many of our suggestions are just "more of the same" good teaching that makes sense for all students, sort of a "double dose" of language. There are some differences, though, in the ways you might use a teaching strategy with ESL learners. For example, in writing a story based on a wordless picture book, native speakers can go directly to writing and illustrating it on their own; ESL learners might dictate a story to someone who writes it in English for them, and then go on to illustrate the dictated story.

GENERAL STRATEGIES FOR TEACHING ESL LEARNERS

Here are some general strategies for teaching ESL learners.

1. Create a rich language environment for all students (see earlier chapters on preschool, kindergarten, and grades one and beyond), but especially for those non-English speaking children who might have had limited exposure to English. Hudelson (1994) uses environmental print as a mirror of the world of English print outside the classroom; "Using environmental print demonstrates a practical application of English reading and writing—to get along in the world" (p. 371).
2. Use centers that encourage lots of talk and listening. Stories on tape are especially useful for ESL learners so they can hear good models of oral reading. ESL learners should have many opportunities to hear English read to them, either on tape or by the teacher, an aide, a volunteer, or an older student.
3. Match more fluent English readers and writers with ESL learners for some activities such as journal writing and talking about a story read to them earlier.
4. Respect and use children's experiences out of school as a bridge to reading and writing instruction. For example, have children dictate and illustrate a personal experience story for someone to record and include it in the classroom library. Include children's books with familiar experiences from cultures of ESL learners. Having some books written in other languages represented in your classroom can be a comforting experience for ESL learners and a valuable awareness activity for native speakers of English who may have never seen sto-

ries in other languages. Honor holidays and special customs of ESL learners, too. ESL learners (and their families) are a great source of multicultural information for you and the other children in the classroom.
5. Label classroom objects in both English and other languages your children speak. Make certain ESL learners, alone or paired with a more fluent English speaker also have significant classroom tasks and responsibilities such as caring for plants or animals, running errands, or selecting a story for the teacher to read.
6. Include simple games such as Bingo or Simon Says and games that ESL learners might bring to the classroom from their cultures.
7. Include lots of easy predictable books for ESL learners. Use the guided or shared reading procedure discussed in the kindergarten chapter to introduce and read these simple books with ESL learners. Repeated readings of these familiar texts build confidence and fluency in all readers, especially ESL learners.
8. Provide lots of vocabulary support tied to an enriching background of experiences needed to read a story or understand a concept. No matter what activity you are doing for ESL learners; they need extra opportunities through discussion and visuals, such as story maps, to understand concepts and vocabulary. Later we present an example of a thematic unit that includes vocabulary practice with key concepts.
9. Be accurate, brief, and clear when you give ESL learners feedback and focus on meaning, not grammar, syntax, or pronunciation. Gersten (1996) suggests giving frequent feedback to ESL learners, asking them to clarify and expand to be understood, giving them tasks they can reasonably complete, using consistent language, and allowing use of native language when appropriate.
10. Find extra hands to help you such as parents and other volunteers, older students, and aides to give ESL learners, that extra practice they need with language.

Our teaching suggestions for the rest of this chapter are organized in two parts: a) the first part deals with using children's literature as a springboard to reading and writing; and, b) the second part deals with helping ESL learners with the vocabulary and content from social studies, science, and other subjects.

Using Children's Literature with Second Language Learners

Teaching Strategies for ALL Learners

Begin by reviewing Chapters 3, 4, and 5 where there are teaching suggestions for using children's literature. These suggestions are good for all children and especially for ESL learners. We urge you to increase the use of these suggestions with ESL learners, especially through extra help using classroom volunteers and aides.

The language experience method allows children to dictate a story and have it recorded by the teacher or another adult, removing the problems some ESL learners have with writing in English. Searfoss and Readence (1994) suggest these steps for completing a story dictation with a small group of children:

1. Children have a common experience such as a recent field trip, classroom visitor, school event, or holiday and then they discuss it with the teacher.
2. The teacher takes rough notes on a chalkboard or chart paper during the discussion, which should be encouraged to go on for as long as children are interested.
3. The teacher makes another draft of the story, with the assistance of the children who help shape it.
4. The children and the teacher reread the story once it is finished.
5. The story is displayed and some follow-up activities planned, such as rereading it later in the day, illustrating it, or placing it in the classroom folder of experience stories.
6. Vocabulary words that carry the meaning of the story can be used to create word games or placed on the classroom list of new words. The teacher can use these words to create vocabulary games and activities later on.

Reading Aloud to ESL Learners

Throughout this book we have urged you to read to children as often as possible and to read a variety of materials to them. ESL learners are no exception; they need an extra dose of being read to by fluent readers who serve as models for them. In addition, Hudelson (1994) suggested that, "Choosing culturally familiar stories seems to be helpful for ESL children, because prior knowledge of characters and/or plots may make the stories more comprehensible to the learners" (p. 379). For the English-only children in

your classroom, hearing stories from other cultures broadens their background of experiences, too.

Literature Response

In recent years, teachers have tried to move away from having children read a story and then answer specific questions about the story as a way to develop comprehension. Unfortunately, this type of question-answer teaching does not always encourage children to dig into a story's meaning and results in children simply wanting to answer the questions correctly. Literature response (or literature study) as we described it in Chapter 5, beginning on page 67, allows all children to share and talk about a story and to relate it to their own lives. You might want to review the steps in literature response we discussed in Chapter 5.

For ESL learners, reader response is especially important. As Hudelson (1994) commented:

> It is not enough to share literature with children. Children, including second language learners, need an opportunity to respond to what they have heard (and later through what they read), to construct meaning, to relate a story to their lives, and to comment on emotion and ideas that a piece evoked. (p. 379)

Mixing ESL learners with more fluent readers of English for some reader response discussions gives ESL learners someone to talk with and they learn from each other as they discuss a story.

Retelling

Retelling is a natural way for children to respond to stories and it is a great replacement for the traditional question-answer format. Brown and Cambourne (1987) presented several types of retelling children can be introduced to, some requiring less language than others. After the teacher reads or tells a story, the children can then retell it orally, retell it in writing, or retell it by drawing. Once children become familiar with retelling stories they have heard, then they can retell stories they have read or written. The *Resources* section lists several sources on using retelling, not only as a teaching strategy, but also as an assessment strategy.

Second Language Learners and Content Area Learning

Many of the teaching suggestions offered for ESL learners are based on using stories and other types of children's literature. But, for many ESL learners, as they move to the middle and upper grades, the challenges of learning social studies, science, and other content concepts becomes overwhelming. The technical vocabulary, endless facts, strange ways in which words are organized, and topics unrelated to their lives differ greatly from the simple story format they are comfortable discussing. Thematic units (similar to those we discussed in earlier chapters) allow ESL learners to experience both content concepts and vocabulary related to a single topic. Next we present a brief outline of a thematic unit on fish, designed to emphasize both the vocabulary and key concepts in the unit.

A THEMATIC UNIT ON FISH

When you think about helping children cope with learning new concepts in a second language, it is a good idea to start with a topic that appeals to the whole class, has lots of visuals, and is fun. We selected the broad topic of fish because children across many cultures are familiar with these colorful creatures. Children may think of some mammals as fish (e.g. whales and dolphins), and some fish as scary (e.g. sharks and manta rays). Children can listen to informational books about fish, they can make and paint various types of fish, sing songs about fish, and go fishing! Nearly every fast food restaurant has fish sandwiches and fish are prepared and eaten in a variety of cultures that steam, sashimi, broil, fry, and barbecue them. Most importantly, there are numerous books about fish and a brief trip to a library with some help from the librarian, and you soon will be filling a large

book bag with great books about fish. Many of these books do a good job of explaining what a fish is, how it survives, and so on. But the language used may be technical and challenging, even for a child whose native language is English. The following teaching strategies should help you to emphasize the use of visuals and repetition needed in learning a second language. The *Resources* section of this chapter contains lists of other resources to expand the unit.

Getting the Fish Unit Started

In order to begin a unit on fish with some idea of the children's background of experiences about the topic, you can start with a think-pair-share activity where they brainstorm and tell a partner words that pop into their heads about fish. You can then record these dictated words on the board or butcher paper as a way of starting the unit.

Children in one second-grade class said the following words about fish:

shark	turtle
frog	aquarium
swimmy	eels
food	dolphins
whale	jellyfish
carp	crab
pescado	Shamu
goldfish	salmon
octopus	trout
shrimp	bass
squid	seahorse
cuttlefish	

Mixing ESL learners with more fluent readers of English gives them all a chance to learn from each other.

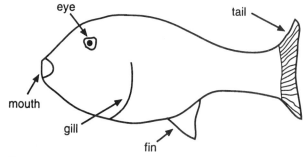

Figure 8.1.

Following this initial activity, it is a good idea to simply make some observations of fish with discussions about what was observed. No texts are used at this point. A field trip to a local aquarium, videos, or observation of a classroom aquarium offers good starting points. In addition to the original brainstorming list, try this activity: Draw a large fish on the board and have the children draw in the parts and label or tell about them. It is only at this point that we are ready to look at some informational books about fish.

The Verbal-Visual Strategy

Most information books about fish have excellent photographs linked to ideas in the text. However, they also can be packed with facts. We recommend reducing the amount of information children have to deal with by focusing on small sections of a text you can read aloud. The key vocabulary in these sections can become part of the words children are trying to learn in the target language. For example, the children's book, *What Is A Fish?* (Snedden, 1993), starts by explaining types of fish with a focus on the largest group, bony fish. The key vocabulary terms in this section include "gills," "fins," and a discussion of how fish breathe and swim underwater. The verbal-visual strategy is a great way to help children personalize their understanding of these technical terms using art as a link to new concepts (Readence, Bean, & Baldwin, 1995). Use the following steps:

The target word to be learned goes in the upper left-hand corner with the definition just below it in the lower left-hand corner. In the upper right-hand corner, children draw or paste in a fish that has "gills." In the lower right-hand corner, they write the name of this fish. The verbal-visual charts can decorate the room as visual aids for other reading and writing activities as the unit progresses. They can also be a part of children's learning logs and a place for posing questions about the topic, such as, "how do gills help a fish breathe?" Rather than books guiding the learning, this approach places the children and the teacher

in charge of exploring the topic based on children's interests. You could get really creative and make a huge fish out of fish scale vocabulary sections children create.

In addition to technical words that students must learn in English, content area books may contain other general vocabulary that mystify students. For example, the book about fish by Snedden (1993) that we mentioned earlier, uses words such as "survive," "fastest," and "powerful." You can have children self-select words from content books that are unfamiliar and make these part of a fun board game designed to encourage risk-taking and verbalization of new words. Board games that resemble familiar game formats, like Candyland, work best and are relatively easy to create. Songs including the words to popular and familiar tunes offer another playful way to help students as they attempt to use new vocabulary. Dramatic play offers yet another vehicle for trying-out new words in the safe haven of a puppet show where the speakers are hidden behind the stage.

Board games like the one that follows, also help children practice unfamiliar words. Make your game generic so you can change the game by merely changing the cards. Word cards can be vocabulary words to be defined, fill-in blanks, or definitions where the child must supply the word. You can give bonuses for the right answer (for example, "move one space"). You can also have cards that ask a student to make movements during the game; such as "make a fish face," "swim like a fish," or "miss a turn." The point is to make your game flexible and adaptable to multiple topics and learning goals.

Comprehension Strategies

Sticking with the idea that second language learners benefit from visual representations of content, there are a number of other ways we can do this. For example, the Herringbone strategy (Dishner, Tierney,

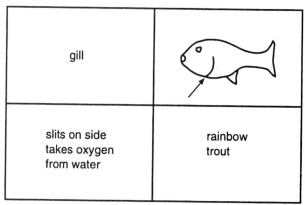

Figure 8.2.

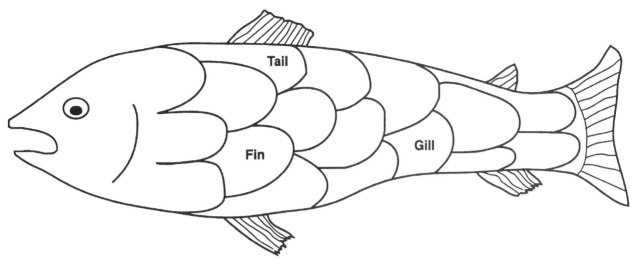

Figure 8.3.

& Readence; 1995) is based on the skeletal features of a herringbone and the five W's of most informational text: who, what, when, where and why (and sometimes how). In the fish unit, children listened while the teacher read them a section of the book, *Facts About Fish* (Bailey, 1990) that described how fish breathe. As she read each important fact, she modeled putting this information in the herringbone diagram that she called "fishbone" for this activity. The children completed this activity in pairs for each of the five W's (and how).

The book mentioned that fish breathe by sucking water into their mouths. The water contains oxygen that is pumped from the fishs' mouths across their gills as blood flows through the gills and brings in oxygen from the water. The children created fishbone diagrams like the one that follows.

The more your visual diagrams can reinforce the topic under consideration, the more second language learners can see connections between the new words and related concepts. To further reinforce this topic you can have the children draw and paint a picture of a fish breathing under water. Crayon pictures with a watercolor wash make beautiful and simple pictures.

Using Art and Song Writing

Origami, the ancient Japanese art form combining drawing, painting, paper cutting, and folding (Miyawaki, 1960) offers yet another concrete way for second language learners to learn content vocabulary and concepts as well as following directions skills. Origami carp can be created by children to decorate the classroom. Carp windsocks are traditionally hung to commemorate the Japanese celebration of Boys Day on May 5th (Miyawaki, 1960). The carp is a symbol of health, vigor, and courage in Japan.

Many cultures assign special significance to creatures like the carp. For example, in Hawaiian culture, the shark is an amakua, or protector for some people. You can have students draw especially powerful creatures from their respective cultures and tell about their symbolic significance. This oral sharing of information can be used in a dictation story you can type for a student to read (Dishner, Tierney, & Readence, 1995). Because the student who dictates the story has cultural knowledge of its structure and significance, learning the English version of the story will be less difficult than a text that is totally unfamiliar. Save this drawing and story in the form of a book and let the student share it with the class.

In addition to the many ways art can be used as a bridge to a new language, songs offer yet another predictable structure that is universally valued. The folk and blues singer Taj Mahal sang a great song that could be used with the unit on fish called, "Fishin Blues," written by Henry Thomas (1968). Here is one of the verses:

	Word	Word		Do		Word	
Do	Word Cards						Word
Do							Do
Finish						Do Cards	Do
Start		Word		Do			Word

Figure 8.4.

The fish sucks water in its mouth. The water goes over the gills. Oxygen gets pumped from the water.

Who? What? Where? When? Why? How?

Figure 8.5.

> *I went on down to my favorite fishin' hole*
> *Baby, grabbed me a pole and a line*
> *Throwed my pole on in, caught a nine-pound catfish*
> *Now you know I brought him home for suppertime*

In the unit on fish, you can have children create a song in pairs or small groups using the words from their giant fish on the wall and the fishbone diagram. You can use popular songs as a rhythmic base for the song you and children create, or you can stick to simple piano and guitar progressions like the one that follows. This song was created by a second grade teacher and his students. The teacher accompanied students on the guitar.

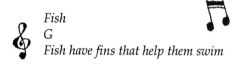

Fish
G
Fish have fins that help them swim

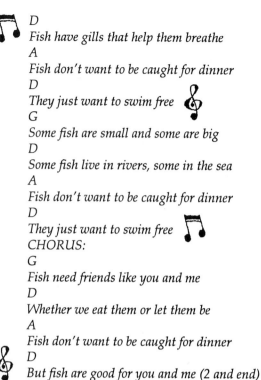

D
Fish have gills that help them breathe
A
Fish don't want to be caught for dinner
D
They just want to swim free
G
Some fish are small and some are big
D
Some fish live in rivers, some in the sea
A
Fish don't want to be caught for dinner
D
They just want to swim free
CHORUS:
G
Fish need friends like you and me
D
Whether we eat them or let them be
A
Fish don't want to be caught for dinner
D
But fish are good for you and me (2 and end)

Using words like "pescado" (fish) you can create songs that include the native language in the chorus (Cockburn, 1995). In addition, if you have computers in your classroom with microphones and speakers attached, children can create a written version of a song in pairs or small groups and perform the song in a recorded fashion on the computer.

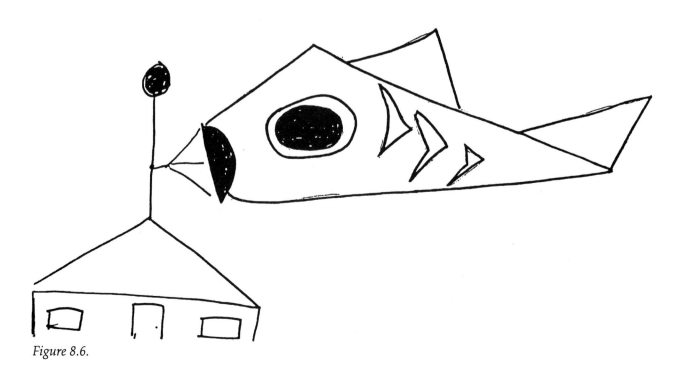

Figure 8.6.

Thematic units based on familiar topics that cross cultures and languages offer ESL learners the opportunity to feel successful as they learn new vocabulary and content in English. The units also offer the same instruction for them as for all learners in your classroom, and give the message to ESL learners that they can learn, too, side-by-side with other children who do not share their gift of a second language.

Summary

We hope this chapter gets you started on how to include ESL learners in reading and writing instruction in your classroom. The strategies we presented are appropriate for all learners, while providing some ways to provide that extra practice ESL learners need. The *Resources* section of this chapter gives you some sources to look into if you want to expand your teaching strategies beyond what we have presented in this chapter.

RESOURCES

Additional Resources For the Fish Unit

There are many books and resources for virtually any topic you plan to teach. Your search may include the library, Internet, and used bookstores. Each of these settings has a treasure trove of materials for ESL students. The materials you and your children develop become additional classroom resources for the future.

Informational Books

Bailey, D. (1991). *Sharks*. Austin, TX: Steck-Vaughn.
Broekel, R. (1982). *Dangerous fish*. Chicago, IL: Children's Press.
Cole, J. (1992). *The magic school bus on the ocean floor*. New York: Scholastic.
Doubilet, A. & Doubilet, D. (1991). *Under the sea from A to Z*. New York: Crown.
Fisher, R. M. (1973). *Namu: Making friends with a killer whale*. National Geographic Society.
Great creatures of the world: Sharks. (1990). New York: Facts on File.
Palmer, S. (1988). *Hammerhead sharks*. Vero Beach, Florida: Rourke.
Parker, S. (1990). *Fish*. New York: Alfred A. Knopf.
Pfister, M. (1992). *The rainbow fish*. New York: North-South Books.
Pfister, M. (1995). *Rainbow fish to the rescue!* New York: North-South Books.

Story Books

Carlstrom, N. W. & Desimini, L. (1993). Fish and flamingo. Boston, MA: Little, Brown, and Co.

Laird, D. M. & Jossem, C. (1981). *The three little Hawaiian pigs and the magic shark*. Honolulu, HI: Barnaby.
Levinson, R. (1988). *Our home is the sea*. New York: E. P. Dutton.
Lionni, L. (1963). *Swimmy*. New York: Scholastic.
Stevenson, J. (1990). *Which one is Whitney?* New York: Greenwillow.
Tokuda, W. & Hall, R. (1986). *Humphrey the lost whale: A true story*. Union City, CA: Heian.
Turnage, S. & Stevens, J. (1984). *Trout the magnificent*. San Diego, CA: Harcourt Brace Jovanovich.

Resources for ESL Teaching ESL Learners

Garcia, E. (1994). *Understanding and meeting the challenge of student cultural diversity*. Boston: Houghton-Mifflin. Chapter 8 of this book is full of practical classroom strategies and some theory about helping ESL students learn content and language. The description of her first-grade classroom by Erminda Garcia is worth finding the book in the library or buying it.
Spangenberg-Urbschat, K., & R. Pritchard, R. (Eds.). (1994). *Kids come in all languages: Reading instruction for ESL students*. Newark, DE: International Reading Association. This little book is a mixture of "how to do it" chapters, information chapters, and some theory chapters on working with ESL learners. Good source for those who want one book that does it all, at least for beginners on the topic of working with second language learners.

Internet Resources for ESL Teaching

You can browse Linguistic Funland for an extensive collection of resource areas in ESL at:

http://www.linguistic-funland.com/teslothr.html

This is a great route to many additional web sites with lesson plans, resource materials, and other teachers sharing ideas.

Books on Retelling

Brown, H., & Cambourne, B. (1987). *Read and retell*. Portsmouth, NH: Heinemann. Easy to read, this text is one of the best written for teachers on the topic of retelling.
Glazer, S. M., & Brown, C. S. (1993). *Portfolios and beyond: Collaborative assessment in reading and writing*. See Chapter 6 on using retellings, both guided and unguided, as an assessment tool. Chapter 5 on think-alouds makes a nice pair of resources on using what children say about what they read to teach and to assess comprehension.

REFERENCES

Bailey, D. (1990). *Facts about fish*. Austin, TX: Steck-Vaughn.
Brown, H., & Cambourne, B. (1987). *Read and retell*. Portsmouth, NH: Heinemann.

Cockburn, V. (1995). The uses of folk music and songwriting in the classroom. In M. R. Goldberg & A. Phillips (Eds.), *Arts as education* (55-66). Cambridge, MA: Harvard Educational Review.

Dishner, E. K., Tierney, R., & Readence, J. E. (1995). *Reading strategies and practices: A compendium* (4th ed.). Boston, MA: Allyn and Bacon.

Garcia, E. (1994). *Understanding and meeting the challenge of student cultural diversity.* Boston: Houghton Mifflin.

Gersten, R. (1996). Literacy instruction for language-minority students: The transition years. *The Elementary School Journal*, 96, 227-244.

Hudelson, S. (1994). Working with second language learners. In L.W. Searfoss, & J. E. Readence, *Helping children learn to read* (3rd ed., pp. 363-391). Boston, MA: Allyn and Bacon.

Miyawaki, T. (1960). *Happy origami.* Hiroshima, Japan: Biken-Sha.

Readence, J. E., Bean, T. W., & Baldwin, R. S. (1995). *Content area literacy: An integrated approach* (5th ed.). Dubuque, IA: Kendall/Hunt.

Searfoss, L. W., & Readence, J. E. (1994). *Helping children learn to read* (3rd. ed.). Boston, MA: Allyn and Bacon.

Snedden, R. (1993). *What is a fish?* San Francisco, CA: Sierra Club Books for Children.

Spangenber-Urbschat, K., & Pritchard, R. (Eds.). (1994). *Kids come in all languages: Reading instruction for ESL students.* Newark, DE: International Reading Association.

Thomas, H. (1968). *Fishing blues.* New York: MCA Music Publishing Co.

CHAPTER 9

Parent
Partnerships

Introduction

Children grow and develop best when home and school work together. Children learn from parents, teachers, and from each other, but it is parents and families who have the greatest responsibility for children's health, safety, and education. Many early childhood experts believe that the happiest and most successful teachers are those who work together with children's parents, other family members, and friends to help children learn (White, Taylor & Moss, 1992; Hildebrand, 1991). We know that parents are interested not only in what happens to their children in day care, preschool and school settings, but also want to know what they can do, also, to help their children learn. Sound working partnerships with parents are based on honest, reliable, and sincere communication between home and school. In this chapter we will make suggestions for how you can build parent partnerships, keep parents informed about children's progress, and provide them with suggestions to help their children succeed in school. The *Resources* section of this chapter has samples of forms, guides, and checklists you can use with parents.

A Day at Thew Elementary School

As you walk from the parking lot toward Thew Elementary School, the first person you meet at the end of the building is a parent volunteer who says, "Good Morning", and points you toward the front office. At the outside door to the office, another parent greets you again and asks if she can help you find your way. Inside the kindergarten classroom we came to observe, a parent volunteer is working in the art center with several children. She tells us that, "This is the best kindergarten in this whole district, my son loves it here. He's the red head over there." A class visit to the library in the afternoon finds several parents working in the library and computer lab, help-

ing children with finding books and using the computers. Later, at the end of our day in kindergarten, notices are given to each child to take home to remind parents that Saturday morning is parent/child computer class in the computer lab. A special school? You bet Thew is special! Richly funded? Not with money, but through the leadership of several talented principals over the years, and the hard work and cooperation of parents, teachers, staff, and children. Thew is a model school to visit if you really want to see parent partnerships in action.[1]

BUILDING PARTNERSHIPS

Getting Communication Started

Partnerships with parents and other family members are based on communication. This communication builds a bond between the home and school and begins even before the children come to day care, preschool, kindergarten, or first grade. Brief telephone conference or conversation before a child comes to your room for the first day, is an important first step in building parent partnerships. The purpose of this first phone call is to introduce the family to you and to tell the parents you want to work with them. If phone calls are not possible, a letter mailed to the home can accomplish the same purposes. The first contact with parents and family should *briefly* explain your expectations for children, give some important details about school routines, and how they can work with you to help their child succeed. A *brief* written report should follow the phone conversation. The time you spend getting materials ready for this written report will be worthwhile since you can use this information over and over, year after year. Some day care centers and preschools develop this information in a brochure for parents. The follow-up written report might include some, but not all, of the following:

Introduction:	Goals and objectives, teacher expectations, organizational procedures, classroom and home learning strategies, and how progress will be reported.
Home Strategies/ Activities:	Provide examples of strategies and activities parents can utilize in the home: provide routines (e.g., reading stories, fingerplays, writing and drawing experiences, homework, etc.)
Materials:	List suggested books, videos, play props that could be used with books and writing
Parent Sources:	Provide resources, parent guide books and brochures

Figure 9.1. Telephone Conference Report Format

Many parents worry about their children's growth and development. Should they be reading? Are they 'normal'? Do all kids throw a ball or write like that? You can share checklists for parents to use as they observe their children at home each day. The *Resources* section of this chapter contains two such checklists. The first one, *Parent Observation List of a Child's Literacy Development*, is a simple way for parents to find out about their children's emerging literacy. The second one, *Developmental Checklist for Parents*, is longer because it assesses many areas of growth (Gelfer, 1991). You should always try to schedule a conversation with parents as they use these checklists to be certain they understand what to look for and to interpret what they find. You can also tell them what you observe at school, using the same checklists.

As part of your first contacts with parents and other family members, you might want to include a general list of suggestions to encourage language at home.

COMMUNICATING CHILDREN'S PROGRESS TO PARENTS

Newsletters, notes, anecdotal records that report what you observe and more formal tests are all ways of regularly communicating children's progress. Some teachers send out weekly or monthly newsletters that contain news of classroom activities and events, stories and poems by the children, notices of upcoming events, and some tips for parents to use at home. Parents also need to understand how important it is to

1. Read to your child as often as possible.
2. Listen to what your child has to say about what he or she has read or written in school.
3. Provide as many books as you can in your home.
4. Get a library card, visit the library with your child, and BOTH of you check out books regularly.
5. Ask your child to retell or draw stories he or she has read orally.
6. Share with your child what you did during your day.
7. Ask your child to share his or her day with you.
8. Check on homework and whether your child needs help with it.
9. Encourage your child to write letters to friends and relatives. Write your own letters to relatives and have the child add a message to each one.
10. Provide a quiet space, no matter how small, for your child to do homework.
11. If space is a problem, try a quiet time when everyone does something quietly.
12. Write together in a family journal or scrapbook.
13. Write stories, shopping lists, and family messages together.
14. Make certain your young child becomes aware of print in the environment such as signs and all kinds of print.
15. Help your child select special words he or she wants to learn and write them on small cards. Keep the cards in a family word box.
16. Post simple messages for your child on the refrigerator or a family bulletin board.
17. Make certain your child sees you writing and reading.
18. Give books as presents.
19. Encourage your child to read and write, and be kind when they make mistakes. Remember, they are just beginners and mistakes are a sign of progress—your child is practicing reading and writing until it becomes easier and easier.
20. Play word games and keep a file of favorite ones to play over and over.

Figure 9.2. Activities for Parents and Children at Home that Encourage Language

It's important for parents to read regularly with children.

read regularly with children. The *Resources* section of this chapter contains a checklist and information sheet to help parents get into the habit of reading with their children at home. *Checklist of Home Reading* is for use by anyone in the home who reads to and with the child. *Information Sheet for Reading to Your Child at Home*, gives tips for what to do before, during, and after reading a story with children.

Finally, it is important that all kinds of reading and writing materials be included in the home. Here are some suggestions you might make to parents. Send them home in a newsletter, one or two at a time so parents can slowly build a language environment at home.

1. Books should be everywhere possible in the home — kitchens, bathrooms, bedrooms — anywhere children spend their time. A place to store books in these areas can be a simple box decorated by the child or a special shelf where books are organized by the child in a way that makes sense to him or her. The more places books are found, the more tempted children are to read. In addition to books, children can add magazines and other kinds of print, such as their own stories to their special book places. Some suggestions for kinds of print are listed below but you will find many more at children's books stores or national bookstores with large children's sections. The children's librarian in your local public library is another valuable person to get to know for suggestions.

2. Early readers also spend a great deal of time and show interest in writing. Providing writing materials for children at home is very important. Things to write with — pens, pencils, markers, and crayons; things to write on — all kinds of paper, big pieces, small pieces, and colored paper can be stored with children's books. A typewriter or a computer can also be used by children to write messages. Magnetic letters and a cookie sheet are an invitation to a child to create a message that can be changed as words are moved around.

3. Parents should encourage and model writing with their children. Working on a birthday card for a special person, shopping lists, an invitation to a party, or a letter to a pen pal makes writing a family event. Keeping a family journal or scrapbook, as we mentioned earlier, is a great way for children to see that writing has real purposes and real rewards.

Parent Conferences

Conferences and workshops are also ways to build partnerships with parents and other family members. The first conferences should be scheduled after about a month or so of school or entrance into a day care center. These conferences are valuable for teachers, parents, and other family members.

Conferences can help *teachers*:

∎ Understand parents and what they expect of the day care or school program
∎ Obtain additional information about the child
∎ Encourage parents to understand and support the program
∎ Determine how the child feels about the program
∎ Communicate the child's progress and talk about his or her development
∎ Supply activities parents can use at home

Books at Home	
Birth to eighteen months:	Concepts books (cardboard, plastic or cloth pages)
Toddler/Preschooler/ Kindergartener:	Nursery rhymes, fairy tales, folk tales picture storybooks, realistic literature, informational books, picture books, alphabet books, number books, poetry, books related to movies, and easy to read books.

Figure 9.3. Suggestions for Books at Home

The conference can help *parents*:

▪ Gain an understanding of the day care or school program and routines
▪ Learn about activities that they can do at home to encourage language growth
▪ Get more information about the teaching style of the teacher
▪ Understand how the child learns and behaves at school

The conference can help *teachers share with parents*:

▪ Lists of recommended books to read to children
▪ Tips and activities for use at home related to topics such as what the child is studying at school, parenting habits, emerging literacy skills, and child growth and development
▪ Learning packets of activities families can do together

Parent Workshops

Teachers can plan short early morning, evening, or weekend workshops for parents and other family members to demonstrate activities and other strategies they can do at home. While written newsletters and lists of helpful suggestions are valuable, sometimes parents appreciate a "hands-on" experience where they can see and practice activities and strategies. Topics will vary with the age of the children, but can include how to make toys and games, constructing puppets, reading to your child, writing with your child, managing difficult behavior, and how to take a trip with your child. Sometimes a workshop can be on a single topic such as emerging literacy, phonics, or attention deficit disorder with information presented by the teacher and another expert on the topic.

If parents cannot attend workshops, try videotaping them and making the tapes available for viewing at home. Include a brief handout with each tape for the parents that tells them what the topic and goals of the workshop are, along with a list of important facts from the tape. Offer them an opportunity to call or stop by and discuss the tape with you when they have time.

Parents and Families Come to School

Parents, grandparents, and other family members should be encouraged to visit their child's classroom and hopefully volunteer some time to help the teacher. A visit to the child's classroom or day care center helps parents really understand your program and daily routines. They also get to see their child work and play with other children. During their visit, offer them

Parents and grandparents should be encouraged to visit their child.

a chance to volunteer some time on a regular basis to help in the room. Sometimes parents and other family members bring special talents you do not have. Grandparents especially are a treasure trove of talents. Their talents can be in art, music, crafts, or assisting children as they learn and play. Here is a list of what parents can do in your room:

What Parents Can Do in the Classroom

1. Read stories to the whole class, small groups or individual children.
2. Listen to children read stories.
3. Write down stories child dictates.
4. Help children with art, music, or play activities.
5. Demonstrate a special talent or skill.
6. Volunteer for class trips.
7. Help with keeping records and general classroom routines.
8. Be that extra hand teachers need during special class plays or other events.

Home Visits

Home visits are usually optional for all kinds of reasons; but sometimes they are a good way to increase communication with parents. These visits should be brief, informal, and arranged with parents who feel comfortable having you in their home. While not always practical, sometimes the extra effort it takes to make a home visit can be very useful as you plan activities for individual children.

Homework

In his wonderful book of poems for children titled, *The New Kid on the Block*, Jack Prelutsky (1984) has a poem about homework that begins, "Homework, Oh Homework, I Hate You, You Stink." Well, that is the reality for many children (funny how adults never seem to remember how they *really* felt about homework when they were in school). Communicating why you give homework, the kind you give, and what you expect them to do with their child to complete the homework are very important steps in making certain homework does not become a chore for everyone. Homework should not be stressful or take too much time for children or parents.

Types of homework can include reading a favorite book with someone at home, writing or drawing pictures to go with a story. Some teachers send a weekly list of homework to parents, such as the one below.

Summary

Building parent partnerships is important for children's success in school. This chapter has pre-sented a few ways to communicate with parents: telephone conferences, newsletters, conferences, workshops, parents come to school, parents in the classroom, home visits, and managing homework. Partnerships are built on regular, honest, and practical contacts with parents and other family members.

Endnotes

1. The authors want to thank the principal, staff, teachers, children, and parents of Flora Thew Elementary School, Tempe, Arizona for creating a wonderful place for learning through parent partnerships.

RESOURCES

Resources for Parents
Parent Observation List of Child's Literacy Development
Developmental Checklist for Parents
Parent Checklist of Home Reading
Information Sheet for Reading to Your Child at Home

Resources for Parents

International Reading Association
800 Barksdale Road
PO Box 8139
Newark, DE 19714-8139

National Association for the Education of Young Children
1834 Connecticut Avenue, NW
Washington, DC 20009

Weekly Homework

Monday: Bring to school, family photographs of your child when he/she was a baby, two years later, and now. We are going to make a family bulletin board and ask your child to draw pictures of what he/she looked like as a baby, now, and when he will go into first grade.

Tuesday: Read "Hungry Caterpillar" to your child.

Wednesday: Write in your School/Family Journal what you will be doing this weekend.

Thursday: Ask your child to teach you the "Five Little Monkeys" fingerplay.

Sign and date each homework assignment you have done together.

Signature and date:

Monday _____

Tuesday _____

Wednesday _____

Figure 9.4. Weekly Homework

National Center for Family Literacy
Waterfront Plaza
325 West Main Street
Louisville, KY 40202

Reading is Fundamental (RIF)
600 Maryland Avenue, NW
Suite 500
Washington, DC 20024

READY*SET*READ Early Childhood Learning Kit
U. S. Department of Education
Washington, DC
1-800-USA-LEARN
http://www. whitehouse.gov/WH/NEW/
ECDC/
http.// www.ed.gov/inits/americareadr/

REFERENCES

Gelfer, J. (1991). Teacher-Parent partnerships: Enhancing communications. *Childhood Education*, 67, 164-167.

Hildebrand, V. (1991). *Introduction to early childhood education* (5th ed.). New York: Macmillan.

Prelutsky, J. (1984). *The new kid on the block*. New York: Greenwillow.

White, K. R., Taylor, M. J., & Moss, V. D. (1992). Does research support claims about the benefits of involving parents in early intervention programs? *Review of Educational Research*, 62, 91-125.

Parent Observation List of a Child's Literacy Development

	Yes	No	Not sure

1. Does your child like someone to read to him/her?

2. Does your child understand what is read to him/her?

3. Does your child understand what he/she reads to him/herself?

4. Does your child pretend to read?

5. Does your child read print in the environment? (e.g., billboards, signs, cereal boxes, etc.)

6. Does your child turn pages of a book properly?

7. Does your child know that print is read from left to right?

8. Does your child retell stories that were read to him?

9. Does your child write?

10. Does your child draw pictures about stories?

11. Does your child like to write?

ACTIVITY

Developmental Checklist for Parents						
Age (mos.)		36-48		46-60		60-72
		Observed	Not Observed	Observed	Not Observed	Observed	Not Observed

I. Motor Skills

A. GROSS MOTOR SKILLS
 Hops on one foot
 Walks on a balance beam
 Jumps rope
B. FINE MOTOR SKILLS
 Builds tower of 9 small blocks
 Copies square
 Cuts out simple shapes

II. Communication Skills

A. SPEECH DEVELOPMENT
 Talks about experiences
 Asks when, how, and why questions
 Communicates well with family and friends
B. VOCABULARY DEVELOPMENT
 Labels actions & objects correctly
 Understands objects in terms of size, shape, & color
 Uses relationship words
C. LANGUAGE DEVELOPMENT
 Carries out a series of 2-4 related directions
 Follows 3 unrelated commands in proper sequence
 Retells familiar story
D. LITERACY DEVELOPMENT
 Shows an interest in reading
 Asks about words around the room or outside the environment
 Can identify several purposes for reading

III. Cognitive Development

A. LITERAL INFORMATION
 Recognizes likenesses and differences
 Names colors
 Names some letters and numbers
B. MEMORY
 Knows last name
 Knows address
 Rote count to 10
C. LOGICAL-MATHEMATICAL KNOWLEDGE
 Stacks blocks or rings in order of size
 Uses tense properly (yesterday, today, and tomorrow)
 Tells time properly

IV. Social-Emotional Development

A. INTRAPERSONAL SKILLS
 Eats, sleeps, toilets without fuss away from home
 Attempts new activities
 Tolerates a reasonable amount of frustration
B. INTERPERSONAL SKILLS
 Shares toys, takes turns with assistance
 Plays cooperatively with other children
 Demonstrates leadership in a group of children

A C T I V I T Y

Parent Checklist of Home Reading

Date _____

Dear _____(Parent's name)_____

Here is a book _____(Child's name)_____ chose from the library today. Please take time to share this book with him or her. When you are finished have your child return the book and this form to school.

Book Title: _____

Please check which sentence applies:

_____ My child read the whole book out loud to me.

_____ My child used the pictures and some words from the story to retell it in his or her own words.

_____ I read this book to my child.

_____ I could not read this book to my child, but someone else did.

_____ We read the book together, taking turns reading.

Comments:

Family member's signature _____

A C T I V I T Y

Information Sheet for Reading to Your Child at Home

Dear Parent(s):

Your support at home will help your child become a successful reader who learns to love reading. Here are some tips for reading with your child at home:

Before Reading

1. Read the title and author of the book or story with your child.
2. Ask your child why he or she picked this book or story to read (almost any reason is a good one!).
3. Take a quick look through the pictures in the book or story.
4. As you look through the pictures, make some predictions. What do you think this story is about? What might happen in the story?

During Reading

1. Read the story to your child or have the child read it to you. Some stories can be shared by each of you reading a page at a time.
2. Stop and chat from time to time about what is happening in the story and how whether your predictions are close to what is actually happening in the story.

After Reading

1. Talk with your child about his or her favorite parts, or parts that were sad, funny, or surprising.
2. If your child enjoyed the book, ask him or her to read it again, either with you or silently, all the way through.